Selected poems of
LÉOPOLD SÉDAR SENGHOR

Selected poems of
LÉOPOLD SÉDAR SENGHOR

Edited by Abiola Irele
Senior Lecturer in French, University of Ibadan

CAMBRIDGE UNIVERSITY PRESS

Cambridge

London · New York · Melbourne

Published by the Syndics of the Cambridge University Press
The Pitt Building, Trumpington Street, Cambridge CB2 1RP
Bentley House, 200 Euston Road, London NW1 2DB
32 East 57th Street, New York, NY 10022, USA
296 Beaconsfield Parade, Middle Park, Melbourne 3206, Australia

First published 1977

Printed in Great Britain at the
University Press, Cambridge

Library of Congress Cataloguing in Publication Data

Senghor, Léopold Sédar, Pres. Senegal, 1906–

Selected poems of Léopold Sédar Senghor.

Bibliography: p.

Includes index.

PQ3989.S47A6 1977   841   76-16919
ISBN 0 521 21339 8 hard covers
ISBN 0 521 29111 9 paperback

CONTENTS

ACKNOWLEDGEMENTS

The Editor is grateful to the following: to President Léopold Sédar Senghor for his cooperation and help in the preparation of the notes and constant expression of interest in this edition of his poems; to Mrs Anne Aderogba of the Cartographic Section, Department of Geography, University of Ibadan, and M. Amadou Faye of the Cartographic Department, Institut Fondamental de l'Afrique Noire (IFAN), Dakar, for their help with the map. To the Editor of *Odu* and University of Ife Press, for permission to include in the introduction to the present volume passages taken from my article, 'Léopold Sédar Senghor as Poet' which appeared in no. 1, New Series, of the review, published in April 1969; to the Publisher and editorial staff of Cambridge University Press, for their forbearance while this edition was being prepared; and to Éditions du Seuil, Paris, for permission to use extracts from the following collections of the poetry of Senghor published by them: *Chants d'ombre, Hosties Noires, Ethiopiques* and *Nocturnes*.

The geography of Senghor's poetry. Léopold Sédar Senghor in his poetry uses various spellings for some names. Therefore the spelling of names on the map will not always agree with spelling in the poetry and notes.

INTRODUCTION

The poetry of Léopold Sédar Senghor is so closely bound up with his career as a politician and ideological leader that the two aspects of his vocation can be considered as complementary poles of the same experience. The poetry is rooted in Senghor's reaction to the colonial situation, in its social, political and moral implications, and to a certain extent can be taken as the imaginative expression of his attitudes and ideas as spokesman of the African cause, and as the principal theoretician and apostle of Négritude. The most obvious character of Senghor's poetry is its overt espousal of African values; it stands in an immediate relationship to a collective experience, and is thus largely conditioned by historical and sociological factors. But it is not only a personal response to these factors, or to his intellectual and spiritual development; it also retraces the essential adventure of an original poetic personality in its contact with external reality; it evolves out of his responses to that reality a singular vision of the world.

LIFE AND BACKGROUND

L. S. Senghor was born in 1906 in Joal, a little town in the Sine–Saloum basin of central Senegal. His father was a wealthy merchant of the Serer tribe, and his mother a Peul (an ethnic group related to the Fulani of northern Nigeria). His maternal uncle, to whom he was very close in his childhood, gave him his early education in the traditional culture, as was customary in a matrilineal society. This was to have a decisive influence upon his future outlook, and he recalls it in these lines from *Chants d'Ombre*:

Tokô'Waly mon oncle, te souviens-tu des nuits de jadis quand s'appesantissait ma tête sur ton dos de patience?
Ou que me tenant par la main, ta main me guidait par ténèbres et
signes?...
Toi Tokô'Waly, tu écoutes l'inaudible
Et tu m'expliques les signes que disent les Ancêtres dans la sérénité marine
des constellations.

Another important influence from these early years was the poetess
Marônne, whose chants introduced him to the traditional literature of
his native area, and gave him his first glimpse of poetry. Senghor's
early childhood seems to have been a sheltered and serene existence
within a closely-knit pastoral community, free of the tensions that he
was to experience later in his contact with a wider world dominated by
the presence of Europe. So he has retained an enchanted memory of
his childhood, which has acquired in his poetry a unique symbolic
value.

Senghor began his formal education at the elementary school in
Joal at the age of seven. This gave him his first encounter with the
French language and Western culture. A year later, in 1915, his father
decided to send him to a boarding school run by Catholic missionaries
in the nearby village of Ngasobil, apparently to remove him from the
indulgent attention of his mother's family. On completion of his
elementary education in 1922, Senghor entered the Collège Liber-
mann, a junior seminary in Dakar, meaning to become a Catholic
priest. He abandoned this plan after six years at the seminary, and
enrolled at the state secondary school, the Lycée van Vollenhoven in
Dakar; but the years of Catholic education have left a permanent
imprint on his mind and personality. It is significant that he contem-
plated entering the priesthood, for the wish reflects the deep religious
sensibility that was later to emerge in his poetry, a preoccupation with
the spiritual side of human experience which is a constant theme of
his cultural and imaginative writings. He completed his secondary
education by obtaining his *baccalauréat* in 1928, and the same year left
Senegal on a government scholarship to study in France, entering the
preparatory class in the Lycée Louis le Grand in Paris in the autumn.

Arrival in Paris was a decisive stage in his emotional and intellectual
development. It brought him into direct contact with France, its
people and culture, and was the beginning of an enduring relationship which, arousing conflicting emotions of attachment and uneasi-
ness, imparted to his writings that note of ambiguity from which they

derive their essential tension. Secondly, he arrived in France in a period of political and social upheavals in France and all over Europe, a situation accompanied by intense intellectual debates and artistic manifestations that reflected the tormented mood of the times. Senghor followed these events closely throughout his student days in France; his writings show that they made a profound impression on his mind as a young African scholar who had previously held a distant and idealised notion of Europe; no doubt they helped to change his view of Europeans and of the relationship between Europe and Africa. Perhaps the most important thing was that Paris was a meeting place for many peoples, and Senghor met students from other parts of the French colonial empire, African, Asian and American (the Caribbean). This contact gave him a wider view of the world and the international situation, and helped to focus his awareness of the colonial question.

Senghor's original intention was to enter the prestigious Ecole Normale Supérieure, but he failed to gain admission, and continued his studies at the Sorbonne, obtaining his *License-ès-lettres* (equivalent to the bachelor's degree) in 1931. A year later followed the *Diplôme d'études supérieures* (the Master's degree), with a dissertation on Baudelaire. In 1935, he passed the highly competitive examination for the *agrégation*. He was the first African to be awarded the degree, and to qualify for it he was obliged to take French nationality. It opened up for him an academic career as a teacher in the lycée, which for the next five years took him to various towns in the provinces, notably Tours in central France and St Martin des Fossés near Paris. During this period he began to write the early poems collected in the volume *Chants d'Ombre*.

At the outbreak of the Second World War in 1939, Senghor was drafted into the French army and saw service on the Northern Front; in 1940 he was taken prisoner by the Germans in the defeat of France. He was interned at various prison camps and spent much of his time in captivity writing the poems that were later to make up the volume *Hosties Noires*. In 1942 he was released on health grounds but confined to Paris, where he took up teaching once more, and in 1944 was appointed Professor of African Languages, at the Ecole Nationale de la France d'Outre-Mer.

The return of peace in 1945 opened up a particularly active period in Senghor's life. He had begun to acquire a reputation in the years before the war through his academic attainments and the essays and articles he had contributed to French publications. The publication in 1945 of his first volume of poems, *Chants d'Ombre*, revealed his talent as a poet, drew attention to his particular concerns as an African, and enhanced his standing in black intellectual circles. He was elected the same year to the French Constituent Assembly as a deputy for Senegal, thus beginning a political career that has been uninterrupted ever since. In 1948 his second volume of poetry, *Hosties Noires*, was published, as well as his historic *Anthologie de la nouvelle poésie nègre et malgache*, to which the outstanding French writer of the day, Jean-Paul Sartre, contributed a preface. In this preface, entitled 'Orphée noir', Sartre presented a critical review of the poetry of French-speaking black writers and attempted for the first time to formulate the concept of Négritude. Another volume, *Chants pour Naët*, which appeared the following year, confirmed the development of Senghor's poetic gifts and established him as a lyric poet of the first importance.

Over the next twelve years, Senghor published only one volume of poems, *Ethiopiques*, which appeared in 1960. His energies were absorbed by politics and by his crusade on behalf of African culture. After the establishment of the Fourth Republic in 1946, Senghor was elected to the French National Assembly as a socialist deputy for Senegal; he later broke with the metropolitan party to found a succession of African parties which he headed at various times in the Assembly up to 1960. He served on numerous commissions in the Assembly and was for a while junior minister in the Cabinet of Edgar Faure. His activities in the French parliament were marked by a ceaseless effort to gain recognition for African rights and attention for African interests, within the context of the colonial relationship. But Senghor did not take the colonial arrangement for granted; he campaigned tirelessly for its transformation, advocating a French Union that would embrace the colonial power and the African territories in a federation of autonomous parts. He conceived this French Union as the model and nucleus of a vaster relationship between Europe and Africa (*Euro-Afrique* as he termed it) in which the essential bond would be mutual respect between civilisations, in an almost spiritual union of peoples who would no longer see each other as antagonistic, but rather as complementary. His political views thus rested on a cultural foundation.

Alongside his political activity, Senghor devoted himself to the promotion of a new understanding of Africa and its civilisation through a constant stream of essays and lectures in France and other parts of Europe, as well as in Africa. He was influential in setting up the review *Présence Africaine* in Paris in 1947 and was one of its earliest contributors, and he was later prominent at the First Congress of Negro Writers organised by the review in Paris in 1958, when he gave the key address. His writings during this period showed a concern to defend the heritage of traditional African culture, and with the definition and promotion of its continuation in the modern world.

In 1958, with the advent of the Fifth Republic, Senghor was appointed *ministre-conseiller* by General De Gaulle who had come to power. But the French Community which De Gaulle inaugurated took a different form from that previously envisaged, and in 1960 most of the African territories which had been members opted for independence. Senegal and the former territory of Soudan came together to form the Federation of Mali, and Senghor became President of the new state. With the break-up of the Federation later in the year, the constituent parts separated, and Senegal became an independent republic under the presidency of Senghor, a position he has held ever since.

Although as Head of State his attention since 1960 has been occupied by political matters and immediate questions of economic and social development – a concern which led him in the early sixties to evolve a comprehensive theory of African Socialism out of the concept of Négritude – Senghor's cultural and literary preoccupations have not taken a secondary significance in his career. He has continued to write poetry and has been instrumental in promoting in Senegal an intense intellectual and artistic life which has made Dakar the cultural capital of Africa, symbolised by the holding there of the World Festival of Negro Arts in 1966. During this new period, Senghor published three more volumes of poetry. In 1961 appeared *Nocturnes* – containing a revised version of an earlier volume, *Chants pour Naët*, and a number of new poems – followed in 1969 by *Elégie des Alizés*, published in a limited edition, and in 1972 by *Lettres d'Hivernage*.

Senghor and Négritude

Senghor's political activity, as a party leader, as a member of the French parliament in the colonial period, and as Head of State of independent Senegal, is an important part of his place in the black world, and his political experience has a direct relevance to his poetry. Even more important has been the role he played in the birth and development of the Négritude movement and in its elaboration as an ideology.

From the beginning of his stay in Paris, Senghor found himself at the centre of a group of African and Caribbean students and intellectuals who had begun to question the colonial system and its ideological foundation, and to reappraise the situation of the black man in the world. This group included Aimé Césaire, who was for some time a fellow student with Senghor at the Lycée Louis le Grand. It was mainly through their friendship and collaboration that what has come to be known as the Négritude movement developed as a distinctive current in the stream of ideas and influences which had begun to flow from French-speaking black intellectuals in the years between the two world wars.

This new consciousness first took shape among black intellectuals in the United States, where the reaction against racial discrimination began to find expression in the political and social ideas of men like W. E. B. Du Bois and Marcus Garvey. Du Bois' book *Souls of Black Folk* was influential in shaping the minds of a generation of younger writers, who started a literary movement now known as the Negro Renaissance, a movement centred on Harlem, the black area of New York City. Among those involved in this movement were the poets Langston Hughes, Countee Cullen and Claude McKay, and later the novelist Richard Wright. The Negro Renaissance in the United States established a tradition of black protest writing which expressed the psychological tensions and social aspirations of black people. As an essential element of the protest theme, this new literature also developed a *mystique* of Africa which focussed the quest of the black American for a cultural and spiritual identity.

The Négritude movement inherited and developed these features of the Negro Renaissance. The younger generation of Haitian writers and intellectuals discovered the poetry and the novels of the Negro Renaissance after the American occupation of their country and took up the racial theme in their own writing. Under the ideological leadership of Jean Price-Mars, whose book *Ainsi parla l'Oncle* played a role in Haiti similar to Du Bois' work in the United States, a French equivalent of the American movement developed in the writings of poets and novelists such as Léon Laleau, Jacques Stephen Alexis, Jean Brière, René Belance, Jacques Roumain and others. This movement has come to be called the Haitian Renaissance, and was the immediate forerunner of Négritude: indeed, a representative selection of the poetry of the Haitians occupied a prominent place in Senghor's 1948 anthology.

The social and intellectual climate in Europe in the years between the two world wars contributed to the growth of the new awareness. The period was notable for its social and political unrest, and for a spiritual ferment, a general crisis of the European consciousness, the aftermath of the traumatic experience of the First World War. Its most important single manifestation was the great economic depression of the thirties, which created enormous social problems and intensified political tensions in virtually all European countries as well as in the United States. Politics and social questions became major concerns, and the literature and thought of the younger generation tended to be dominated by a left wing radicalism which reflected the bitter and restive mood of the times. In political and social philosophy, as a result of the Russian Revolution in 1917, Marxism began to exert an influence beyond the circle of its avowed adherents and gave an impetus to the spread of socialist ideals. In the arts, surrealism called into question the traditional canons of thought and expression and expressed the quest for new and deeper values. Both movements represented a wide-ranging criticism of the prevailing order in the West, and the elaboration of a new conception of man's place in society and the world.

Young black intellectuals followed these movements and read the principal works of their exponents, which gave a powerful incentive to criticise Western society and culture, and to reappraise the political and social framework of the colonial relationship and the moral and spiritual values of the culture of their colonial masters.

Of particular importance in the development of Senghor's ideas was the work of the French conservative writers and thinkers who sought to combat radical movements by creating a French national *mystique* based on tradition and the Catholic religion. The vigorous

affirmation of the French national spirit in the poetry of Charles
Péguy and Paul Claudel, in the writings and activities of Charles
Maurras and Maurice Barrès, whose phrase 'la terre et les morts'
summarises the spirit of the movement, is akin to the awakening of a
similar consciousness in Senghor. He knew their work and his own
writings show this influence on his conception of history and culture
as determinants of racial and national communities.

As part of the intellectual revolution taking place in Europe, the
development of anthropology favoured the emergence of a new
self-awareness on the part of the black intellectuals. The notion of the
inherent superiority of the white race was undermined by the growth
of a 'relativist' attitude to the study of culture, which showed non-
Western cultures to be functional within their own settings. This
attitude encouraged a new appraisal of African societies, values and
arts, and a new understanding of African people. The German
anthropologist Frobenius wrote his *History of African Civilisation*
during this period, and Senghor became acquainted with the work
through a French translation published in 1936. Among the French,
the work of Maurice Delafosse, Robert Delavignette and Marcel
Griaule contributed to a better appreciation of African societies and
cultures. At the same time African art had a vogue in artistic circles in
Paris, through the influence of African sculpture on leading Parisian
artists, such as Picasso, Braque and Modigliani.

These various influences left strong traces in the writings of black
writers, and in particular of Senghor. Black intellectuals from the
USA and the Caribbean and from Africa had found a meeting point
around the journal *La Révue du Monde Noir* founded by two sisters,
Paulette and Jane Nardal, both from Martinique, who ran a literary
salon for black writers and intellectuals in Paris in the late twenties
and thirties. In 1921 René Maran, a black writer from Martinique,
published the novel *Batouala,* based on his experience as an adminis-
trator in the then French Equitorial Africa; some passages criticised
French colonial rule. The novel won the prestigious Prix Goncourt
and the publicity drew attention in France to the colonial problem. In
1932 a young Martinican, Etienne Lero, started a paper *Légitime
Défense* whose first and only number contained a violent attack on
French colonial policy and its demoralising effects on the black
personality. So by the time Senghor arrived in France there was
already a strong current of feeling in black intellectual circles. Sen-

ghor involved himself in these activities, and in collaboration with Léon Damas, Aimé Césaire, and Birago Diop founded the journal *L'Etudiant Noir* which began to feature articles on race and on African culture. During this period, in 1939, Césaire published his long poem *Cahier d'un retour au pays natal*, in which the word 'Négritude' first appeared in print. Senghor had begun already to publish the series of essays in which his ideas on Africa and the black race began to unfold, and at the same time to try his hand at poetry.

The Second World War delayed the emergence of a full-blown movement from these early activities; but after the war most of the people involved were reunited once more in Paris. In 1947 Alioune Diop, a Senegalese, founded the review *Présence Africaine*, which provided a forum for black writing, and by 1948, when Senghor's anthology appeared, the literary work of French-speaking black writers had evolved such a unity of theme and coherence of expression as to constitute a distinctive literary school. Jean-Paul Sartre was thus able to dwell upon this common element in his essay 'Orphée Noir', to examine in particular the concept of Négritude in which it was summed up, and to attempt to draw out its significance. By 1956, when the First Congress of Negro Writers and Artists was held in Paris, Négritude had become the focal theme of all Senghor's writings, and the subject of a debate among black intellectuals – indeed a controversy, that has hardly abated today.

Among its various uses by different writers, it is necessary to distinguish two broad senses of the term 'Négritude'. It can be taken to mean either the historical movement of French-speaking black intellectuals (and more narrowly the literary school that grew out of it), or the concept of a basic element that underlies the personality of black men and determines a fundamental sensibility, a collective ethos, of the black race. The first meaning carries merely the implication of an awakening of the black consciousness to the realities of the black man's historical condition in the modern world, and in particular, of the colonial situation. As Aimé Césaire put it: 'La Négritude, c'est la simple reconnaissance du fait d'être noir, et l'acceptation de ce fait, de notre destin de noir, de notre histoire et de notre culture.'

It is this recognition and this acceptance to which the literature of Négritude gives expression. Though the works of French-speaking black writers have the diversity of the temperaments and outlooks of their authors, they revolve around a number of characteristic themes that define the limits of their literature and give it a unity. These themes range from the revolt against colonial domination in its political, cultural and moral aspects, to a defence and revaluation of Africa and its people and culture, and the cultivation of a *mystique* of the black race. The central motivation of this literature can be seen as the quest of a Westernised and alienated black élite for an identity, and in consequence their effort to affirm their racial belonging.

The second meaning of Négritude derives from this latter aspect, for the quest for identity gives rise to the notion of a distinctive spiritual heritage of the black man. Senghor has been responsible for the elaboration of this notion into a theory that has marks of a philosophical system. Some of the leading ideas of Senghor's theory are discussed later in relation to his poetic practice; for the moment, it can be noted that these ideas are worked out in an effort to present a comprehensive view of African civilisation and values, and to relate these to a unified conception of the black race.

Négritude has a close relationship with other political and cultural movements among black communities in the Americas and in Africa, and can be considered as the francophone equivalent of Pan-Africanism; it is related to the idea of 'African personality' developed in English-speaking Africa. It is one manifestation of black nationalism, marking the desire of black people to change the conditions of their historical relationship with the West, and a preoccupation with the destiny of the black race in the modern world.

The poetry of Senghor has an important position in the literature of Négritude and in its content and attitudes exemplifies the themes and characteristics of black poetry in this century. But if in this sense the poetry is typical, it expresses an individual feeling for life which transcends its attachment to a collective cause, and reflects a preoccupation with human experience that is more fundamental and therefore more properly poetic.

Senghor has drawn on his rich and varied experience of cultures to compose a personal poetic idiom and vision. His outlook on the world was fashioned to a great extent by his African background. The pastoral environment in which he grew up as a child has been mentioned; the influence of local customs and traditions can be felt in his poetry through direct allusions and often in the tonalities that give his verses their peculiar quality. Senegal has been an important meeting point of peoples and cultures, in direct touch over many centuries with various currents of civilisations, and this has created in the poet a sensitivity to history that implies a broad view of humanity. As he writes in one of his poems:

> J'ai poussé en plein pays d'Afrique, au carrefour des castes, des races et des routes.

Thus the historical vision in Senghor's poetry embraces the collective life and personality of his native region and of Africa, and extends into a wider perspective.

Inevitably his profound assimilation of Western culture constitutes another essential element in his poetry, complementing his African background. Senghor's formal education was classical and literary; he developed a strong attachment to the authors he studied and found in the French poets models for his own efforts. But he brought to these models a response conditioned by his background and his needs, so his preferences have gone to those poets whose works he could relate to an African sensibility. The dominant influence on his poetry has been exerted by poets who sought to penetrate through the diverse manifestations of the sensible world to an essential unity in a fundamental life of the universe. This intention lies behind the theory of 'correspondances' hinted at by Baudelaire in his sonnet of that title in *Les Fleurs du Mal*. Senghor integrated the idea into his own theory of Négritude. Baudelaire's immediate successors, Verlaine, Rimbaud and Mallarmé carried forward his innovations into new developments that determined the temper of modern poetry in French as indeed in other European languages: a poetry that relies on symbolism to express complex sensations and a more profound perception of realities that lie behind the social and natural references of traditional French poetry. The influence of Baudelaire and Verlaine upon Senghor is direct, and his poetry reflects their evocative manner and expressive musicality. The spiritual orientation of Baudelaire's poetry and that of the Symbolist poets culminated in the Surrealist movement headed by André Breton, and though Senghor's poetry owes little in style and manner to Surrealist poetry, the ideas of the movement entered into his thinking and poetic practice. He has sought to translate into an African register the Surrealist view of life with its appeal to the inner forces of consciousness and quasi-mystical conception of reality.

But the most important influence on Senghor's poetry is that of

Paul Claudel, who gave the mystique of nature a specific application in an organic poetry that celebrates the mysteries of the Catholic faith. Claudel's powerful temperament found expression in an ample verse form which allies the movement of modern free verse to the cadences of the Bible. This verse form, known as the *verset*, was taken over by Senghor, who infused into it elements of the oral poetry of traditional Africa.

These and other influences from the French tradition – such as the poetry of Péguy and St John Perse – indicate that an important dimension of Senghor's poetry derives from developments within French literature, to which it is obviously related both by language and by much of its informing spirit. These influences have been fused into an individual idiom; the direction of Senghor's poetry is towards the development of an African sentiment and vision in a poetry whose medium of expression remains French. As he once said, commenting on the work of the first generation of French-speaking black poets: 'Notre ambition est modeste: elle est d'être des précurseurs, d'ouvrir la voie à une authentique poésie nègre, qui ne renonce pas, pour autant, à être française.'

Senghor's poetry can thus be considered a pioneer enterprise, standing at the head of a modern African imaginative expression.

THE POETRY

Senghor's life and political career, and his role in the black intellectual and cultural renaissance, are the background concerns that have determined the themes of his poetry. But it is also essential to see how these concerns become art, which takes them beyond their immediate historical reference, and are developed in a poetic expression that expresses the consciousness of an individual.

Senghor's poetry relates to the broad historical framework whose outer limits are defined by the relationship between Africa and Europe, felt in the first instance as an opposition between two races and their conceptions of life. This opposition is the starting-point of Senghor's poetry and determines in a fundamental way all his expression. But it also acquires immediate personal significance in its direct pressure upon his experience as an individual; consequently, in his poetry, it assumes an intense symbolic value. So although the poetry has the primary interest of reflecting the impact of a collective situation upon an individual consciousness, it also conveys the reverse movement of the poet's mind and sensibility into a broad area of human experience, in its historical and social manifestation as well as its profound spiritual implications. The peculiar intensities of Senghor's poetry result from the constant tension between his 'social' individuality and his deeper poetic self, and from his effort to transcend an implied opposition between the two. So the poetry expresses the adventure of a sensitive temperament in its exploration of experience and its aspirations towards a comprehensive vision of life.

Chants d'Ombre, Hosties Noires

This begins to unfold in the two early volumes, *Chants d'Ombre* and *Hosties Noires*. Both are centred primarily upon the external reference of the poet's experience, and contain poetry that is 'public' in content and in the postures adopted by the poet. Senghor is more concerned in these volumes with the revelation of his personal responses to the pressures of external reality, in an immediate historical and social sense, than with a statement of his insights into the general human condition.

The poems of *Chants d'Ombre* are a kind of mental diary of his experience of exile in Europe. They are marked by his feeling of solitude, by an acute sense of a radical dissociation between the individual self and the European environment. These poems arise out of an immediately felt condition of psychological disturbance and spiritual disorientation in a highly sensitive individual, with a heightened capacity for introspection. His insight into his ambiguous position in a social and moral universe to which he can relate by reason of his intellectual assimilation but from which he feels himself divorced in his deepest emotions, leads to the intense and often uneasy self-consciousness of the poems of *Chants d'Ombre*. It also explains his insistence upon his difference, in terms of race and also of mental disposition and spiritual constitution.

Out of this awareness of his apartness the poet gropes towards a sense of his identity. In the poem 'Le totem' we glimpse the process through which the conflict at the social plane gives rise to the psychological drama of identity – the poem expresses the cleavage between the social consciousness of the poet and his intimation of an inner being, the *malaise* of the *assimilé* astride two worlds. The feeling of inhibition and frustration that this situation generates can be felt more in the tone of a poem like 'Ndessé ou Blues', which suggests that Senghor may have lived this situation as a personal dilemma, and indeed as a deep neurosis.

These poems are thus 'confessional' in their correlation of direct experience with their author's subjective states. They recall in their pervading mood the melancholic dissatisfaction in nineteenth-century French poetry, the *ennui* of the Romantics, and the 'spleen' of Baudelaire. The feeling of profound alienation from the world of men, affecting the poet's attitude to the living reality of nature, which in the French poets often appears as a striking of attitudes, sometimes leads Senghor to strike a sentimental note, but the sentiment itself is saved from vulgarity because his poetry dramatises in direct and appropriate imagery a state of mind that is concretely felt. Moreover, the imagery developed in meditation on the alienated condition has a significance beyond the personal reference. The individual sense of loss and solitude is the apprehension of an existential plight, a metaphysical anguish felt to be inherent in the human condition.

In its symbolic representation, it is a meditation that remains particularised. The physical separation from Africa is a drama of the individual removed from the familiar environment of his native country and is also symbolic of a more profound estrangement, that of the soul from the roots of its being:

Et cet autre exil plus dur à mon coeur, l'arrachement de soi à soi
A la langue de ma mère, au crâne de l'Ancêtre, au tam-tam de mon âme...

The theme of exile is thus central to *Chants d'Ombre* and underlies all the other themes, as well as the attitudes revealed, in the whole of Senghor's poetry.

The complementary aspect of this theme is the poet's nostalgic quest for his origins, the psychological return to Africa. One can see in this theme the expression of a simple reaction to the pain of the European experience, a means of compensation and self-justification. Africa is presented as a counter to Europe, and this determines the poet's attitude to his native continent. In his exile, he draws moral sustenance from the memory of an earlier life, transformed in his imagination into an anterior state of grace, so that the image of Africa is coloured by the associations of a childhood experience of security and primal innocence. As he puts it in one of his poems:

J'ai choisi ma demeure près des remparts rebâtis de ma mémoire, à la
    hauteur des remparts
Me souvenant de Joal l'Ombreuse, du visage de la terre de mon sang.

The focus of these associations naturally becomes his natal village which he evokes in ecstatic terms in the poem 'Joal', and to which he refers in other poems as the ultimate point of reference of his African belonging and sentiment.

It would be reductive to see the African theme in Senghor's poetry as merely a compensatory device; it carries implications beyond its psychological significance. In the first place, it makes a valid effort at self-affirmation, a deliberate movement of the heart and mind towards a unified experience of the self. The evocation of childhood memories in 'Joal' serves not merely to create a source of emotional comfort, but also to establish the sense of a firm belonging, of a participation in a way of life essential to his own being:

> Seule, je sais, cette riche plaine à la peau noire
> Convient au soc et au fleuve profonds de mon élan viril.

More than the quest for harmony dictated by a momentary exile, the African theme registers the broader affirmation of the reality of the poet's African antecedents, of a historical and spiritual continuity which is the informing principle of his individual identity. It is this realisation of the enduring quality of his heritage that the poet expresses in the address to the masks:

> Vous distillez cet air d'éternité où je respire l'air de mes Pères.

The communion of the living with the dead is the very essence of the spiritual life of Africa, so devotion to the ancestors is a marked form of dedication to the continent. Here the secondary theme of survival makes its appearance; it is a theme with a particular significance in Senghor's imagery and symbolism. It begins to receive some elaboration in *Chants d'Ombre*, but the most marked characteristic of the volume and the explicit intention of the African theme is the revaluation of Africa, and its role in affirming the poet's sense of community and self-identification, through a celebration of the values that animate African life. The inspiration of poems such as 'Prière aux masques', 'Nuit de Sine' and 'Que m'accompagnent kôras et balafong' proceeds from understanding communal existence as a spiritual destiny, of history as essentially a working-out within the community of a vital relationship between man and the natural environment. The individual, participating in the life and values of the community, is also involved in the larger relation with the forces of creation. The force of Senghor's dedication to Africa and to this view of the collective existence is best conveyed in the poem 'Femme noire', the affective charge with which he invests his personification of the continent and thus transforms the image he presents into the governing symbol of a significant poetic myth.

Senghor's sense of community is rooted in an intense historical consciousness and derives from the intimate association in his mind between the individual destiny and the spiritual progress of the community. The African theme provides the primary channel of expression for this consciousness, but it is a theme that develops as the culmination of a psychological process. *Chants d'Ombre* documents the stages of this process. In it, we witness the poet's efforts to take the measure of his situation and to work out the terms of his relationship to the world. At the same time, the direct reciprocity between the social personality and the imaginative self of the poet begins to extend its range of significance in his identification with his ancestors, so that the African image becomes the central focus of his imagination. It moves away from its first polemical significance – his feeling of dis-illusionment with the European experience – towards a more general affirmation of an authentic mode of life. Africa becomes both the racial homeland and a poetic mode of envisaging the world and man's relation to the universe.

Senghor's first volume defines a line of thematic progression from the social and psychological to the imaginative and visionary which the other volumes may be said to develop and amplify. The same progression is implicit in *Hosties Noires,* though the social and political emphasis is more pronounced. The poems here are the most 'com-mitted' in all his work, by their direct reference to the historical events that led to the Second World War. The date of composition of nearly every poem is given, so it is easy to see how they span the uneasy years before the war and the period of the war itself, and bear wit-ness to Senghor's experience of the European crisis and his response to it. The volume is divided into two parts, 'Ethiopie' and 'Camp 1940', to reflect the two phases of the crisis covered by the volume. The Italian invasion of Ethiopia in 1938 marked an important stage in the events that led to the Second World War, and was an indica-tion of Africa's involvement in the European conflict; while Senghor's captivity and internment show his direct experience of the war.

The poems of *Hosties Noires* can be seen as a comprehensive *critique* of Europe. Because they are in a strict sense war poems, they provide a specific moral viewpoint for Senghor's appraisal of the contradictions of Western civilisation. They are a commentary on public events as well as a judgement on the human passions behind those events, through which Senghor attacks the European claim to superiority over the rest of the world. So, the poems present an ironic reversal of roles for the colonised black, who now sees himself in a position to set up a moral watch on the white master.

The critique of Europe and the note of protest are suggested in the title. It suggests the sacrifice of Africans to the blind fury of the European war, in the context of a colonial domination of which the African is a victim, and which is itself the sign of a fundamental moral insufficiency in the white man. The association also has a religious overtone which conveys a secondary meaning, that of the collective passion of the black race, conferring on it the nobility of suffering. *Hosties Noires* is conceived out of an opposition between Africa and Europe, victim and aggressor, dramatically represented in the poem 'A l'appel de la race de Saba'. The poet's public concern becomes an explicit commitment to the race, giving voice to its grievances against the white and to its hopes of liberation and fulfilment. As he says:

> Qui pourra vous chanter si ce n'est votre frère d'armes, votre frère de sang?

The protest theme expresses itself not as a documentation of these grievances and the formulation in poetry of a programme of political action, but as a passionate defence of the black race, and a systematic exaltation of its virtues and moral stature set against the moral collapse of Europe. The poems 'Camp 1940', 'Lettre à un prisonnier' and 'Taga de Mbaye Diôb' are devoted to this theme, and reveal a concern to project a new image of the race that is only by implication ideological. This produces that lack of a sharp edge to the protest theme in Senghor, in marked contrast to that of other black poets – to the militancy of David Diop's poetry, for example. Difference of temperament might explain the contrast, but it is more significant to consider the deeper moral intention behind the poems of *Hosties Noires*. Senghor can criticise the political pretensions of Europe and draws attention sufficiently to the horrors she is capable of unleashing within and beyond her frontiers, but his interest and emphasis throughout are centred upon the agony of men involved in the European war, its moral implications. His essential preoccupation is the inability of European civilisation, for all its vaunted superiority, to create and sustain a humane order among men, and it is from this viewpoint that Europe is condemned and Africa presented as a counterpoise. Thus in 'Chant de printemps', the picture of Europe exhausted by war and drained of its spiritual energy is complemented by the vitality of Africa, agent of renewal and harbinger of a new universal order.

So in *Hosties Noires* the African image takes on its clearest polemical complexion in Senghor's poetry, expressing a public vocation for the poet in the cause of his people. The Africa–Europe antithesis is not only historical and political, but more profoundly moral and spiritual. But the 'interested' character of this image also leads to an extreme idealisation, that never attains the richness of his evocations in other volumes, and so remains too simplified to carry conviction.

Senghor's commitment in *Hosties Noires* has another characteristic which requires stressing. Despite its explicitness, it is affected by a singular ambivalence of his feelings towards Europe and in particular France. At the heart of this commitment lies a conflict of emotions which lends a poignant force to his criticism of Europe, as in 'Neige sur Paris' and 'Prière de paix'. Senghor's cultural and emotional attachment to France is expressed in these poems with a candour that reveals the paradox of his individual situation. For the appeal of the humanist ideals of French civilisation remains too strong with him, and its intellectual and literary traditions run too deeply in him to permit a total and untroubled rejection of what he owes to his French education, even in his rejection of Europe. It is less with resentment than with sorrow that the poet expresses his sense of betrayal. This mood also contributes to the subdued character of his protest, and gives a note of compassion to his evocation of the ravages of war on the French.

The ambivalence in Senghor's poetry corresponds to an acutely felt perception of his own dilemma as a man of two worlds, a complex of attitudes and emotions which he renders with singular sincerity in his poetry. Yet its importance is not that it diminishes his sense of loyalty to Africa, but determines a direction of his feelings towards a resolution of his personal conflict. Senghor feels the necessity, in the very grip of this conflict, to reaffirm his African belonging:

> Mère, sois bénie!
> Reconnais ton fils parmi ses camarades comme autrefois ton champion,
> *Kor-Sanou!* parmi les athlètes antagonistes

A son nez fort et à la delicatesse de ses attaches...
Reconnais ton fils à l'authenticité de son regard, qui est celle de son coeur
et de son lignage.

At the same time, he seeks in his poetry to carry his consciousness
beyond the antithesis created by the colonial situation and to elaborate a new ideal of unity that would embrace both terms of reference
of his cultural and human awareness. He seeks a reconciliation of
Africa and Europe, and also defines the universal brotherhood that
he envisions at the end of the volume:

Et donne à leurs mains chaudes qu'elles enlacent la terre d'une ceinture de
mains fraternelles
DESSOUS L'ARC-EN-CIEL DE TA PAIX.

'Prière de paix' sums up the significance of *Hosties Noires*. The
European war is seen as a holocaust consuming the earth, as
Apocalypse in which Africa takes the aspect of a redeeming force, and
the black poet that of prophet of a new hope for mankind.

Ethiopiques, Nocturnes

There is a perceptible change in Senghor's poetry after the first two
volumes; it is felt as a new inflection of his themes and a corresponding modulation of his expression into a new register. One could
simplify by saying that Senghor abandons the public manner; cer-
tainly the tone of the poetry becomes more private as the inspiration
appears less overtly related to the colonial experience and Senghor's
immediate response to it.

This change is prefigured in the more intimate style of the group of
poems with the collective title 'Par delà Eros' that forms the final
section of *Chants d'Ombre*, and in the impressionism of poems like
'Mediterranée' and parts of 'Chant de printemps' in *Hosties Noires*. It
becomes fully revealed in the sequence of love poems entitled *Chants
pour Naët* published as a single volume in 1949, and later revised and
incorporated under the title *Chants pour Signare* in *Nocturnes*. This
group of poems reveals Senghor as a lyric poet, turning towards a
deeper exploration of the poetic self and developing a more complex
and more varied attitude to the world than his public posture allows
in the first two volumes. This evolution is confirmed in the poems of
Ethiopiques, and in the *Elégies* which, apart from a long sequence
'Chant de l'initié' and a couple of other pieces, are the only new
poems in *Nocturnes*. If then, in the first two volumes, Senghor is
concerned essentially with giving voice to an individual predicament

as part of a collective historical plight, in the poetry that follows his vision appears to be projected beyond the historical and circumstantial, to embrace a wider universe of experience.

This is not to say that the public personality of the poet disappears in *Ethiopiques* and *Nocturnes*, for it remains the ultimate determining element of his view of the world. Even at its most lyrical, Senghor's poetry is never wholly centred upon a world of private experience, for the collective reference of his work and the African sentiment from which it proceeds defines a first state of consciousness that underlies and orients all his expression. Indeed, in a number of poems in the later volumes, the poet returns to the specific question of his public situation, to explore the psychological drama entailed in the relationship between his social consciousness and his poetic sensibility. In 'Le Kaya–Magan' and 'L'absente' (*Ethiopiques*) and 'Elégie de Minuit' (*Nocturnes*), Senghor poses the problem of his dual status as individual engaged in the concrete reality of public life and as poet, whose profound inclination is towards the contemplation of the obscure, immaterial life of the universe. In the section 'Epîtres à la Princesse' of *Ethiopiques*, he returns to the Africa–Europe antithesis to work out in his personal relationship with a white woman a new mode of reference to Europe which both accommodates and justifies his African identity. The essential preoccupation in these poems is the fusing of the poet's duality into a single will and consciousness. The more reflective tone of these poems results in a new lyricism and an attenuation of the declamatory and rhetorical style of the first two volumes, and in the greater subtlety of the imagery and expressiveness of the symbolism.

The themes of *Ethiopiques* and *Nocturnes* flow from the concerns of the earlier volumes. The feeling of alienation, expressed as a personal concern for survival, now formulates itself as a preoccupation with the idea of regeneration, as an obsession with a personal sense of vigour that draws directly upon the force of nature for its maintenance. So 'Femme noire' in *Chants d'Ombre* leads directly to 'Congo' in *Ethiopiques*, in which the poet's image of the black woman is given elaboration in a procession of sensual images that relate primal eroticism to the very movement of the universal life. The same quest for vitality is expressed in 'Le Kaya-Magan', where the poet conflates the image of a historical personage with an ideal of himself, establishing a correspondence between the social awareness and spiritual consciousness that are aspects of his own duality; through this correspondence he aspires to a higher cosmic sentiment and purpose:

> Car je suis les deux battants de la porte, rhythme binaire de l'espace, et le
> troisième temps
> Car je suis le mouvement du tam-tam, force de l'Afrique future.

Similarly, Senghor's personal sense of contradiction underlies the structure of 'A New York' in its presentation of opposites, and his quest for inner coherence dictates the movement of the poem towards reconciliation in a unity of experience.

The way in which the personal aspect of Senghor's poetry gives his general vision its particular intensity is best illustrated by the transformation through which the sequence of love poems *Chants pour Naët* acquires a new dimension in its later version as *Chants pour Signare*. Senghor's revisions bear mainly on the style, and apart from the omission of direct references to 'Naët', these do not affect the substance of the poems to any significant extent. They remain a comprehensive hymn of praise to the poet's loved one, who embodies his image of the black woman as well as his spiritual ideals. While the poems retain the emotional tone of the earlier attachment which inspired them, their more general reference to the black woman as symbol rather than as a particular individual emerges in the later versions with greater clarity. The transformation was possible because Senghor's themes and the imagery that expresses them relate to several levels of feeling at the same time. He is thus able to employ the same sensual evocation of the black woman to express an individual attachment and also a sense of filial devotion to Africa and a dedication to an imaginative ideal. These various associations attached to his image of woman, and grounded upon a theme of social responsibility, inform the poem 'L'Absente' and give it its peculiar complexity.

The element of self-consciousness in the first two volumes also provides the constant emotional base of the poems of *Ethiopiques* and *Nocturnes*, expressing itself in a somewhat more introspective style. The grave and often sombre atmosphere of the *Elégies* in the latter volume show how a reflective tone has come to control the earlier self-dramatisation, how the poet's self-awareness has now diffused itself in a more intimate identification with the elements of his imaginative universe. This process is mediated by Senghor's African sentiment, on which his feeling for the world ultimately rests.

Senghor envisages the world from a perspective defined by Africa in two ways. As the original home of the poet's soul, it is the 'royaume d'enfance' and carries associations of spontaneous living and freshness of vision. The poetry is a conscious means of recovering an original personal heritage. And as an extension of this, Africa becomes a poetic landscape, 'Ethiopie', a spiritual universe suggestive of a fundamental apprehension of the world.

The bond between the individual and his environment, which in the earlier volumes had the notional function of clarifying the poet's identity, here takes on a new dimension: it indicates the organic and fundamental situation of man within the enduring cycle of the natural order. This larger vision finds its most significant elaboration in Senghor's imagery and symbolism.

Imagery and symbolism

Since Senghor's poetry is largely a conscious realisation in poetic terms of an individual feeling for the values of his African background, we need to consider the body of ideas through which he has sought to elucidate these values, and which constitute his theory of Négritude. We reach in this way an appreciation of the role of image and symbol in his poetry.

Senghor sees Négritude as a complex of attitudes and dispositions which make up the collective personality of black people and determine their unique outlook on the world. This unity of the black personality is rooted in a common African origin, which provides a cultural and spiritual foundation for all forms of collective expression. The social organisations and modes of life found in Africa have common characteristics which distinguish them and give them fundamental unity. African survivals in the New World have left an imprint on the personality and way of life of Afro-Americans, so that African culture is a unified reference for the black personality, for a cultural and spiritual universe that makes a 'black world'. Blackness, or Négritude, resides essentially in the participation, immediately or at a second remove (as in the case of the Afro-American) in a fundamental African spirit of civilisation. Thus Senghor has defined Négritude as 'l'ensemble des valeurs du monde noir'.

The outstanding trait of the black man, for Senghor, is his unusual capacity for feeling, 'l'émotion'. The African has a heightened awareness of life which enables him to communicate with the world of nature and to respond in a dynamic way, with all his being, to its inner promptings. This emotive disposition is manifested in his intense sense of rhythm, and leads on the spiritual plane to a mystical attitude to the world which finds expression in African animism. For the traditional societies of Africa assume an underlying unity of the world, which binds all the parts together in a vast system of 'correspondances'. The world itself is permeated by the presence of the dead, and by a certain essence of life, embracing the manifest and the unseen, which constitutes a spiritual reality to which the African is attuned, and which he apprehends intuitively. Senghor refers to this higher order of reality, after Breton, as 'le surréel'; in the African context this implies strong awareness of a divine presence in the natural world, a conception of the universe as sacred.

The African's sensuous grasp of the world gives a profoundly religious character to life in the traditional culture. African civilisation is governed by a sense of communion between men, and between man and the environment; and collective life is regulated by social activities and ceremonials which maintain a constant awareness of the sacred. Myth and ritual thus form important elements of the expressive schemes of African societies.

Senghor has sought consciously to assimilate his own poetic practice to this view of African civilisation. For him, artistic creation is a privileged mode of the African apprehension; and poetry, because of its intimate link with ritual, is a sacred activity. The poetic image does not merely register sense impressions or convey in metaphor relations between aspects of experience and of external reality; it expresses a deeper spiritual feeling, and reveals a fundamental order of the universe.

Senghor's images are concrete and often sensuous, but move in their appeal beyond physical perception to an evocation of the inner significance of their immediate references. This gives an impressionistic quality to Senghor's poetry, which relies for effect more on the feeling it induces and the atmosphere it creates than on rational understanding.

> Vert et vert le Printemps au clair mitan de Mai, d'un vert si tendre ho! que c'est ravissement...
> C'est la tendresse du vert par l'or des savanes, vert et or couleurs de l'Absente.

The association of greenness with growth and renewal combines with the warmth of gold and the luminous perspectives of the savannah at midday to produce a splendid effect. The meaning of the lines inheres in the evocation, rather than in literal statement. Similarly the scene-setting in the opening lines of 'Nuit de Sine' conveys the quality of mystery with which the African night is suffused rather than a pictorial presentation. Senghor's images function as clusters of associations and suggestions which intensify their effect and deepen their meaning. The distinction between image and symbol is blurred, and Senghor himself has expressed a preference for what he calls 'l'image analogique', which is a concrete equivalent of an essential quality of things rather than a descriptive representation, because for him such an image establishes a closer equivalence between spheres of experience, and reflects more adequately the intimate association between physical sensations and the illumination of the mind which emerges from them:

L'Esprit germe sous l'aine, dans la matrice du désir

The multivalence and symbolic resonance of Senghor's images proceed from his characteristic inclination towards primary sensations, and to his preoccupation with an intensity of experience that finds expression in the constant engagement of his imagination with organic images. The universal images in his poetry are manifestations of an essential vigour running through the whole of creation, and in which man is profoundly involved:

Et de la terre sourd le rythme, sève et sueur, une onde odeur du sol
    mouillé
Qui trémule les jambes de statue, les cuisses ouvertes au secret
Déferle sur la croupe, creuse les reins tend ventre gorges et collines
Proues de tam-tam.

The procession of imagery gives a vitality to Senghor's evocation that often belies the sinuous movement of his lines. Whole complexes of association and perspectives of meaning are built around simple images which acquire new values from their contexts. An image such as 'rosée' carries multiple connotations progressing from freshness to that of lustral element, agent of purification. In the following lines, which conclude 'Lettre à un prisonnier', Senghor states more than a personal hope, he suggests a universal renewal:

J'attends ta lettre à l'heure où le matin terrasse la mort noire.
Je la recevrai pieusement comme l'ablution matinale, comme la rosée de
    l'aurore.

The image of blood in particular has a special significance: it forms the central reference in a cluster of symbolic notations indicative of an insistent vitalism in Senghor's poetry. Apart from denoting the poet's sense of his communal ties, it also registers his preoccupation with a life force. Thus 'sang sombre', 'lait noir', 'vin noir' are related images denoting an essence of life, associated with an intensity of being whose ultimate direction is a passionate exaltation of the elemental:

Surgisse le Soleil de la mer des ténèbres
Sang! Les flots sont couleurs de l'aurore.

Blood also has a connection with the image of woman. Senghor's attachment to this image has a psychological implication as well as a symbolic significance in its reference to Africa. The eroticism that often goes with his evocation of woman is not mere sensual gratification; it conveys the idea of sexual union as a sacramental act, as a form of participation in the rhythm and creative force of the universe. Woman is thus imagined in terms of procreation and perpetuation of the race, fertility and regeneration – in short, as a cardinal principle of life. The association of the image with the poet's continent gives it a further dimension – through this image, Senghor develops in his poetry a scheme of vital values that inform the celebration in these lines to the Congo:

Oho! Congo couchée dans ton lit de forêts, reine sur l'Afrique domptée
Que les phallus des monts portent haut ton pavillon
Car tu es femme par ma tête par ma langue, car tu es femme par mon ventre
Mère de toutes choses qui ont narines, des crocodiles des hippopotames
Lamantins iguanes poissons oiseaux, mère des crues nourrice des moissons.
Femme grande! eau tant ouverte à la rame et à l'étrave des pirogues...

These lines bring out admirably the way in which the African scene provides the material of Senghor's attitudes and the foundation of his poetic thought. The concrete portrayal of Africa as a landscape in the luxuriance of natural growth is centred upon the symbolic connotation of water as a seminal element, and develops into the image of Africa as a source of being, thus operating an intimate identification of the continent with the poet's entire universe of feeling and of vision.

Senghor himself has pointed out the particular importance the African references in his poetry have for him.

Et puisqu'il faut m'expliquer sur mes poèmes, je confesserai encore que presque tous les êtres et les choses qu'ils évoquent sont de mon canton:

quelques villages *sérères* perdus parmi les *tanns*, les bois, les *bolongs* et les champs. Il me suffit de les nommer pour revivre le Royaume d'enfance – et le lecteur avec moi, j'espère – 'à travers des forêts de symbôles'.

The image of Africa in Senghor's poetry is formed out of a conscious recall by the poet of his antecedents, charged with a newly developed feeling for the mode of life they elaborate. And because his evocations refer to a particular physical landscape and environment to which his earliest and most enduring memories are attached, they not only give a concrete quality to his experience and localise his expression, but also define his mode of perception. This direction of the African identification emerges clearly in the specific use that Senghor makes of elements of African myths and symbolic schemes to give depth of meaning and even a ritual dimension to his own poetry. The constant recourse to organic and especially vegetal imagery is an indication of a consciousness formed by an agricultural society, and shows the same kind of preoccupation with growth, with an immediate sense of the surge of life in the natural world, characteristic of an animist outlook, to which Senghor's deepest poetic inclinations approximate. The identification of the moon with the female principle and with fertility, which is a development of this category of imagery, belongs to the same order of consciousness and finds in Senghor's poetry parallel meanings which enrich his evocations of the night star. More significant still is the widespread symbolism of the serpent which carries in most African societies complex associations which combine a sexual meaning – deriving from the identification of the serpent with virility – with its symbolic representation of strength and clairvoyance. In such terms as 'serpent de la mer' and 'serpent de l'eau' and particularly in the notation 'oiseaux-serpent', Senghor employs the symbol to express the link between the physical and the intellectual, the fundamental insight into the processes of life that makes for total experience.

It is not the literal correspondence of Senghor's imagery and symbolism with African systems of thought that is important, but their transposition and integration within an individual poetic apprehension. Beyond the allusions to his native customs and to elements of African cosmology, Senghor's imagery and symbolism build up a poetic mythology expressive of an intense responsiveness to the natural world, of a full sense of life:

Ma fore s'érige dans l'abandon, mon honneur dans la soumission
Et ma science dans l'instinct de ton rythme.

Africa thus acquires a central significance in Senghor's poetry as the reference of his experience, the most natural channel of his poetic intentions and as the prime mediator of his imaginative vision: 'Il m'a donc suffi de nommer les choses, les éléments de mon univers enfantin pour prophétiser la Cité de demain, qui renaîtra des cendres de l'ancienne, ce qui est la mission du poète.'

The visionary significance of the image of Africa is seen in Senghor's symbolism of *night*, which derives its special importance from the association with Africa and with blackness. Night can be considered the governing symbol in Senghor's poetry, as he said himself: 'Je proclame la Nuit plus véridique que le jour'. It represents the authentic mode of the black poet's imagination. The importance of this symbol in Senghor's poetry can be explained as a deliberate intention to reverse the negative associations of blackness in European culture. Africa, 'le pays noir', assumes a value in line with the rejection of European canons of judgement and the effort to revalorise African civilisation, and this effort affects the black poet's attitude to the European language he employs and to his imagery and symbolism.

Night is opposed to day, as black to white. It is associated with peace and meditation, with the propitious presence of the dead and with the mystic life of the continent. Its essential value is underlined in the poem 'Mediterranée' in which Senghor presents Africa, 'au delà de l'oeil profane du jour', and assimilated to the 'rythme nocturne de la terre'. The immediate association of night with blackness also extends to the colour blue, which is endowed with a mystic quality:

Et les toits se penchent écoutent, les étoiles sourient de leurs yeux sans
    sommeil
– Là-haut, là-haut, leur visage est bleu-noir.

The opposition of night to day is however not systematic in Senghor's poetry. Indeed he often endows the day with a value that complements that of night. Dawn shares some of the quality of night, while at the time heralding new life. As a progression on this connotation of dawn, Senghor's vitalism is consistently expressed in images related to the daytime, for while the night produces an atmosphere of calm repose, the day implies activity and movement, the surge of the life force. Thus Senghor employs images of light and of bright colours to express the full intensities of being. The day at its high point signifies ecstatic revelation, a sense of exaltation as in the opening lines of 'Femme noire', and the image of light itself corresponds to a mood of spiritual illumination:

> Mais lumière sur nos visages plus beau que masques d'or.

Senghor has devoted much of his poetry to the grave sombreness and mystery of night, and has earned the title 'poète de la nuit', but he is also a poet of brilliant and resplendent evocations.

The complementary character of day and night also attests to his constant desire for the reconciliation of opposites, and illustrates his conception of nature as a pattern of various elements held in harmony by a fundamental sympathy. The intimate expression of this conception gives effect to the opening lines of *Chants pour Signare*:

> Une main de lumière a caressé mes paupières de nuit.

Day and night form a couple that belongs to an order of complementary entities in the universe, which includes other couplings like man and woman, earth and sky. Though differentiated and even sometimes opposed, their alternation is analogous to the rhythm of the world. Moreover, these couplings are not exclusive to each other, but form part of a network of interactions, and it is in this coupled relatedness of various elements and aspects of the universe that the very processes of life are maintained. To relate in a dynamic way to another being is thus to participate in this process of reciprocation, in the movement of life:

> Car comment vivre, sinon dans l'Autre, au fil de l'Autre, comme l'arbre
>   déraciné par la tornade et les rêves des îles flottantes
> Et pourquoi vivre si l'on ne danse l'Autre?

Here we find a cardinal principle of Senghor's theory of Négritude – the idea of subjective identification with other beings as a form of participation in the essence of the universe, which he ascribes to the African. In the poetry, the conception loses the partisan character which lingers in the theory; it becomes an ideal of the poetic function, the revelation of an original quality of nature which the poetic image renders immediate to the consciousness:

> Voici revenir les temps très anciens, l'unité retrouvée la reconciliation du
>   Lion, du Taureau et de l'Arbre
> L'idée liée à l'acte l'oreille au coeur le signe au sens.

These lines sum up the purport of Senghor's Négritude and define the framework of the poetic mythology within which his imagery and symbolism are inscribed. They give direction to the poet's attachment to an active cultivation of the values of life, which find their meaning, their profound value, in opening the human sense and spirit to a comprehensive quality of experience.

Style and versification

Basically, Senghor's poetic style derives from the French tradition, and it is not difficult to identify in his work specific influences and affinities with French poets. A line like this indicates the direct influence of Baudelaire and his symbolist successors:

Et le soir tombe, sanglot de sang qui libère la nuit.

Nonetheless there is evidence of his conscious approximation of the structure of French poetry to his African subject matter. This has a consequence for his poetic method which cannot be ignored. Within the framework of the French prosodic tradition, Senghor has incorporated into his versification African elements, either similar to or different from the resources of his borrowed medium, and the union forms a personal idiom.

Senghor's choice of verse form is instructive. He employs free verse, in the strict sense of the French *vers libre*, which consists of combinations of the different verse forms or of segments of the classical alexandrine. This gives varying combinations of syllabic groups, determined in each line or within the movement of whole sections of the verse by the accentuation which, as is usual in French poetry, coincides with pauses. Senghor's lines generally divide into regular groupings on a binary principle, and even where the syllabic count is irregular, each section of his verses tends to respond in its actual movement to this principle. The dominance of the alexandrine is apparent in Senghor's versification, as this example from *Hosties Noires* demonstrates:

Et mon père étendu sur des nattes paisibles, mais grand, mais fort, mais beau.

In this picture of his father, Senghor employs a pure alexandrine in the first part of the line, which he then reinforces with a half-alexandrine having three marked accents to emphasise his father's physical attributes. Senghor can also vary his effects to create a different pattern for a different effect:

Trés pieux, / pour les faons / de mon flanc, // les residents / de ma maison / et leurs clients.

In this line, in which the assonating words *pieux* and *clients* both have two syllables, Senghor pairs off three word-groups with three syllables, with three other word-groups having four syllables, the first group balancing the second in a neat and clear pattern, and the whole line being held together by the interplay of alliteration and assonance. In another line, an exceptional use of *vers impairs*, distributed evenly into four sections, gives a striking effect to a prophetic evocation:

> Les plus beaux épis / et les plus beaux corps // élus patiemment / parmi mille peuples?

It is obvious that Senghor's versification does not involve a total liberation from the set forms, but rather a freer deployment of the resources of the French poetic tradition to construct within the movement of his verses significant units through which his thoughts and feelings are developed. His lines are built up as periods, which accounts for their broad, expansive flow, and the suppleness of his versification renders it more capable, despite its deliberate organisation, of adapting itself to different themes, situations and moods.

What is most significant about Senghor's poetic method is the way in which he has sought to make consistent use, within the general framework of French poetry, of the formal traits generally associated with the oral poetry of pre-literate societies, and with the traditional poetry of Africa in particular.

Perhaps the most distinctive illustration of this process in Senghor's poetry is his systematic use of repetition, in various forms, as a cardinal principle. The recurrence of the same or similar words, of phrases or of similar figures within sections of his poetry can create an impression of monotony that his French critics have been quick to notice and to condemn. But the use of repetition has important functions in his poetry, and is one of his most effective borrowings from oral tradition, for it serves as a real principle of organisation in his verse, as a ground-bass for the progression of his ideas or of his feelings. This function of repetition appears in its most simple manifestation when it is used as a refrain, as the phrase 'Mère, sois bénie', at the head of each stanza of the poem, 'A l'appel de la race de Saba'. In this poem, the figure of Africa as a mother in distress, readily suggested by the historical reference of the poem, is merged with that of the poet's own mother, and this correspondence is transmitted throughout the poem by the refrain. Repetition is used as a leitmotive maintaining at intervals the emotional colour of his poems. It also serves as a device to anchor the rhythm of the variously patterned succession of his lines, less in a strictly metronomic than in a logical sense. This function of repetition appears most clearly when the repeated element stands at the head of the line, with each recurrence prompting a new flow of ideas and images:

> Ecoute le bruissement blanc et noir des cigognes à l'extrême de leurs voiles déployées
> Ecoute le message du printemps d'un autre âge d'un autre continent
> Ecoute le message de l'Afrique lointaine et le chant de ton sang!
> J'écoute la sève d'Avril qui dans tes veines chante.

In the same way he uses repetition to establish the final resolution, the mood of confidence at the end of a spiritual agony in the poem 'Elégie de minuit':

> Viendra la paix viendra l'Ange de l'aube, viendra le chant des oiseaux inouïs.

Repetition is employed in poetry, especially by practitioners of free verse, to impose organisation on their verse-form, and the similarity of Senghor's procedure to that of Claudel and St John Perse suggests the general interest of Senghor's method. Its particular interest derives from the fact that repetition is the principle which underlies another important characteristic of his poetry, the use of enumerations and of parallelisms, the succession or juxtaposition of related figures and images, which he has taken directly from African oral tradition, especially the praise poem (though the European reader will see similarities with the oral poetry of the Bible). It is interesting to compare the following extract from Igbo tradition with a passage from Senghor's poetry:

> I am
> The Camel that brings wealth
> The Land that breeds the Ngwu tree
> The Performer in the period of youth
> The Back that carries its brother
> The Tiger that drives away the Elephants
> The Height that is fruitful*...

Consider now the following passage from 'Lettre à un poète':

> Tu t'allonges royal, accoudé au coussin d'une colline claire,
> Ta couche presse la terre qui doucement peine

* Romanus Egudu, 'Ojebe Poetry', *Black Orpheus*, no. 21 (April 1967), 7-14.

Les tamtams, dans les plaines noyées, rythment ton chant, et ton vers est la
respiration de la nuit et de la mer lointaine.
Tu chantais les Ancêtres et les princes légitimes
Tu cueillais une étoile au firmament pour la rime
Rythmique à contre-temps; et les pauvres à tes pieds nus jetaient les nattes
de leur gain d'une année
Et les femmes à tes pieds nus leur coeur d'ambre et la danse de leur âme
arrachée.

Senghor's eulogy to Aimé Césaire follows the same pattern as the
Igbo poem, and has a formal interest in the way the poet constructs
a series of praise attributes around the noble figure of Césaire as
variations on the same idea stressed and developed with each repetition.

Exactly the same principle is at work in the litany of praises which
the poet addresses to his ideal of the African woman in the middle
section of his well-known poem, 'Femme noire':

Femme nue, femme obscure
Fruit mûr à la chair ferme, sombres extases du vin noir, bouche qui fais
lyrique ma bouche
Savane aux horizons purs, savane qui frémis aux caresses ferventes du
Vent d'Est
Tamtam sculpté, tamtam tendu qui grondes sous les doigts du Vainqueur
Ta voix grave de contre-alto est le chant spirituel de l'Aimée.

Femme nue, femme obscure
Huile que ne ride nul souffle, huile calme aux flancs de l'athlète, aux flancs
des princes du Mali
Gazelle aux attaches célestes, les perles sont étoiles sur la nuit de ta peau
Délices des jeux de l'esprit, les reflets de l'or rouge sur ta peau qui se moire.

Here the principles of enumeration and repetition are more subtly
applied, particularly in the last line of the quotation in which they are
deftly combined, each attribute enumerated by the poet shifting
forward and running into the next as an extension of the same image.
The effect of this kind of procedure in which repetition and parallelism weave a series of variations on a basic theme though the poem is
often to quicken its pace, and to give it a real progression which
contributes to its cumulative impact.

The influence of the African praise poem further explains Senghor's predilection for the forms of direct address, which determines
the frequent occurrence in his poetry of the apostrophe and the
vocative, as in the opening lines of his 'Prière aux masques'.

Masques! O Masques!
Masque noir masque rouge, vous masques blanc-et-noir
Masques aux quatre points d'où souffle l'Esprit
Je vous salue dans le silence!

The incantatory character of this opening is heightened by the obsessive recurrence of the apostrophe in a way which recalls African religious chants. Senghor's poems are in the main eulogies addressed to individuals, or invocations addressed to the forces of nature. His method can be compared with the practice of his immediate predecessors in the French tradition, Claudel and St John Perse, who revived in their own poetry the earlier tradition of praise poetry in European literature, and Biblical and liturgical forms. The derivation of Claudel's *Odes* from religious laudations and litanies, and of St John Perse's *Eloges* from their secular heroic and courtly versions, reminds us that much poetry had direct sacred or social functions and applications in early societies, and still does in the traditional literature of present-day African societies. The possibility that the two French poets may have exerted an influence on Senghor in this matter cannot be excluded, yet it would be improper to speak of imitation. Senghor was quite aware of the African tradition, in particular that of his own region, as his theoretical writings on the subject show.* It would be more correct to speak of the convergence in his poetry of two related traditions, the African manner exercising at least as much an influence as the French poets who were his masters, and whom he sought to parallel by referring his own method directly to his own background.

The work in which Senghor's appropriation of the African tradition is most evident is his 'Taga de Mbaye Dyôb', a poem which is a direct adaptation of the Senegalese praise chant (*taga*) associated with the griots (praise-singers) and chanted to the accompaniment of a drum (*tama*, also prescribed by Senghor for his own poem).†

Where Senghor is not adapting a form borrowed from the African tradition, his conception of poetic expression remains oral or, as he has put it, 'auditive'. An essential element in the internal organisation of his poetry is the preponderant role of sound values in creating its total effect. 'Je persiste à croire,' writes Senghor, 'que le poème n'est

* See in particular the essay 'Comme les lamantins vont boire à la source', appended to *Ethiopiques*.

† See Notes pp. 112–13 for more detailed consideration of the poem.

accompli que s'il se fait chant, parole et musique en même temps.' His poetry is notable for its 'musical' conception, and almost every page of his work abounds in expressive sonorities which give it its characteristic sensuous flavour. The interplay of these sound effects with the other aspects of his technique underline further the oral character of Senghor's poetry.

The auditory element is an important part of any poet's method, for all poets rely on the sound values of the words they put together. In the case of Senghor, it is specially important because it is closely bound up with his whole approach to poetic creation. If Senghor seems to verge on excess in his use of effects of tone and timbre and repetition of sound values, he makes more systematic use of them because of his intention to give his written poetry the oral quality which literature still retains in Africa, to create a poetry which comes immediately and dramatically alive as the spoken word.

The simplest manifestation in Senghor's poetry of the use of sound qualities is the straightforward imitative effect, or onomatopeia, as in this example:

> L'Europe m'a broyé comme le plat guerrier sous les pattes pachydermes des tanks

– where the plosives combine with the image to render in acoustic terms the idea of the war and the elephant-like movement of the tanks. Here the device is employed with more significant effect to realise concretely and graphically a visual image:

> Oh! écoute quand glissent glacées d'azur les ailes des hirondelles migratrices

Rhythm and sound combine in yet another evocation to intensify the expression of an important idea:

> Nous sommes les hommes de la danse, dont les pieds reprennent vigueur en frappant le sol dur.

This constant concern for sound effects, which produces the wealth of alliteration and assonance in Senghor's poetry, is also structural, for it reflects the poet's concern with pattern. One of the clearest examples of the purposeful use of alliteration as a connecting link is found in his 'Taga de Mbaye Dyôb' where two series of related words are paired off and highlighted by the repetition of similar sounds and also by the regular distribution of syllabic quantities in a line made up of two alexandrines:

Et que les accompagnent les cordes des kôras! Et que les accompagnent les
vagues et les vents!

Senghor uses alliteration here to distinguish between the homage
of men, indicated by the musical instruments, and the participation of
the elements in this homage to Mbaye Dyob. Again, a particularly rich
effect is obtained by the use of alliteration in the concluding line of
another poem of homage:

Paroles de poupre à te parer, Princesse noire d'Elissa

Having the resources of the French language at his disposal,
Senghor has taken full advantage of them and has worked into his
poetry a whole range of effects which gives it the character of a
balanced system of cadences and of harmonies. He has forged a
personal style by the integration of the formal structure of French
poetry, and the intrinsic quality of the French language itself, with
elements borrowed from the oral poetry of his native land, so rendering more adequately his individual feeling for the African universe
that he explores.

Reference has already been made to his adoption of the *verset*
developed in French by Claudel, and familiar to English readers in
the poetry of Whitman. A more rounded view of Senghor's diction
would be to see it as a combination of the direct and rhetorical
expression of the French Romantics (Victor Hugo comes readily to
mind) with the allusive and elliptical manner of the moderns established by Baudelaire. Thus Senghor's versification has tended from
the beginning towards a style of ceremonial. His prosody and verbal
technique are based on an apparent simplicity of form and language,
which is offset by the complexity of his symbolism, and the multiple
character of the associations which adhere to his more effective
images.

This observation points to the essential purpose of Senghor's poetic
style. The poem is conceived by him as a deliberate construction, a
vehicle of thought and feeling as well as a manner of perception. It is
realised as a dramatic medium, in which the poet's experience and his
response to the external world are exteriorised and made palpable
with the help of the verbal resources offered him by language. There
is a direction in his poetry towards the total conception of artistic
expression of the oral traditions of pre-literate societies, a concern to
endow the spoken word with its original value and quality in the
traditional cultures of his African background, to insert it within a

whole system of symbolic representation, involving the whole being. His 'return' to Africa thus becomes inherent in his very poetic method:

> Mais si'l faut choisir à l'heure de l'épreuve
> J'ai choisi le verset des fleuves, des vents et des forêts
> L'assonance des plaines et des rivières, choisi le rythme de sang de mon
> corps dépouillé
> Choisi la trémulsion des balafongs et l'accord des cordes et des cuivres qui
> semble faux...
> J'ai choisi mon peuple noir peinant, mon peuple paysan, toute la race
> paysanne par le monde.

The significance of Senghor's poetic language reveals itself as a purposeful orientation of the resources of his medium towards the expression of a specific mode of feeling and vision. His turning to Africa implied for Senghor a revision of his attitude to the world, involving his espousal of African values; also an adaptation of his means of expression to the mode of experience which underlies these values, and to which, through image and symbol, he endeavours in his poetry to give a new form and meaning.

SELECT BIBLIOGRAPHY

Poetical works

Poèmes (Comprising in one volume *Chants d'Ombre, Hosties Noires, Ethiopiques, Nocturnes, Lettres d'Hivernage*). Paris, Editions du Seuil, Collections Points, 1973.
Elégie des Alizés, Paris, Seuil, 1968.

Prose

Liberté I: Négritude et Humanisme, Paris, Editions du Seuil, 1964.
Liberté II: Nation et voie africaine du socialisme, Paris, Editions du Seuil, 1971.

Edition

Ndiaye, Papa Gueye. *Ethiopiques: édition critique et commentée*, Dakar, Nouvelles Editions Africaines, 1974.

Criticism

Bâ, Sylvia Washington. *The Concept of Négritude in the poetry of Léopold Sédar Senghor*, Princeton. Princeton University Press, 1973.
De Leusse, Hubert. *Léopold Sédar Senghor l'Africain*, Paris, Hatier, 1967.
Guibert, Armand. *Léopold Sédar Senghor, l'homme et l'oeuvre*, Paris, Présence Africaine, Collection Approche, 1962.
Guibert, Armand. *Léopold Sédar Senghor*, Paris, Seghers, Collection Poètes d'Aujourd'hui, 1969.

Mezu, S. Okechukwu. *Léopold Sédar Senghor et la defense et illustration de la civilisation noire*, Paris, Didier, 1968.

Mezu, S. Okechukwu. *The Poetry of Léopold Sédar Senghor*, London, Heinemann Educational Books, 1973.

Van Niekerk, Barend. *The African Image in the Work of Senghor*, Cape Town, A. A. Balkema, 1970.

Biography and general

Crowder, Michael. *Senegal: A study of French Assimilation Policy*, 2nd edn, London, Methuen, 1967.

Hymans, Jack. *Léopold Sédar Senghor, An Intellectual Biography*, Edinburgh, Edinburgh University Press, 1972.

Kesteloot, Lilyane. *Les Ecrivains noirs de langue française*, Brussels, Institut Solvay, Université Libre de Bruxelles, 1963.

Kesteloot, Lilyane. *Négritude et Situation Coloniale*, Yaoundé, Editions CLE, 1970.

Milcent, Ernest and Sordet, Monique. *Léopold Sédar Senghor et la naissance de l'Afrique moderne*, Paris, Seghers, 1969.

Mortimer, Edward. *France and the Africans, 1944–60*, London, Faber, 1969.

THE POEMS

Lettre à un poète

A Aimé Césaire

Au Frère aimé et à l'ami, mon salut abrupt et fraternel!
Les goélands noirs, les piroguiers au long cours m'ont fait goûter de
tes nouvelles
Mêlées aux épices, aux bruits odorants des Rivières du Sud et des Iles.
Ils m'ont dit ton crédit, l'éminence de ton front et la fleur de tes
lèvres subtiles
5   Qu'ils te font, tes disciples, ruche de silence, une roue de paon
Que jusqu'au lever de la lune, tu tiens leur zèle altéré et haletant.
Est-ce ton parfum de fruits fabuleux ou ton sillage de lumière en
plein midi?
Que de femmes à peau de sapotille dans le harem de ton esprit!

Me charme par delà les années, sous la cendre de tes paupières
10   La braise ardente, ta musique vers quoi nous tendions nos mains et
nos coeurs d'hier.
Aurais-tu oubliée ta noblesse, qui est de chanter
Les Ancêtres les Princes et les Dieux, qui ne sont fleurs ni gouttes de
rosée?
Tu devais offrir aux Esprits les fruits blancs de ton jardin
– Tu ne mangeais que la fleur, récoltée dans l'année même, du mil fin
15   Et ne pas dérober un seul pétale pour en parfumer ta bouche.
Au fond du puits de ma mémoire, je touche
Ton visage où je puise l'eau qui rafraîchit mon long regret.
Tu t'allonges royal, accoudé au coussin d'une colline claire,
Ta couche presse la terre qui doucement peine
20   Les tamtams, dans les plaines noyées, rythment ton chant, et ton vers
est la respiration de la nuit et de la mer lointaine.
Tu chantais les Ancêtres et les princes légitimes
Tu cueillais une étoile au firmament pour la rime
Rythmique à contre-temps; et les pauvres à tes pieds nus jetaient les
nattes de leur gain d'une année
Et les femmes à tes pieds nus leur coeur d'ambre et la danse de leur
âme arrachée.

25   Mon ami mon ami – ô! tu reviendras tu reviendras!
Je t'attendrai – message confié au patron du côtre – sous le kaïcédrat.

Tu reviendras au festin des prémisses. Quand fume sur les toits la
    douceur du soir au soleil déclive
Et que promènent les athlètes leur jeunesse, parés comme des fiancés,
    il sied que tu arrives.

Nuit de Sine

Femme, pose sur mon front tes mains balsamiques, tes mains douces
    plus que fourrure.
Là-haut les palmes balancées qui bruissent dans la haute brise
    nocturne
A peine. Pas même la chanson de nourrice.
Qu'il nous berce, les silence rythmé.
5   Ecoutons son chant, écoutons battre notre sang sombre, écoutons
Battre le pouls profond de l'Afrique dans la brume des villages
    perdus.

Voici que décline la lune lasse vers son lit de mer étale
Voici que s'assoupissent les éclats de rire, que les conteurs eux-mêmes
Dodelinent de la tête comme l'enfant sur le dos de sa mère
10   Voici que les pieds des danseurs s'alourdissent, que s'alourdit la
    langue des choeurs alternés.

C'est l'heure des étoiles et de la Nuit qui songe
S'accoude à cette colline de nuages, drapée dans son long pagne de
    lait.
Les toits des cases luisent tendrement. Que disent-ils, si confidentiels,
    aux étoiles?
Dedans, le foyer s'éteint dans l'intimité d'odeurs âcres et douces.

15   Femme, allume la lampe au beurre clair, que causent autour les
    ancêtres comme les parents, les enfants au lit.
Ecoutons la voix des Anciens d'Elissa. Comme nous exilés
Ils n'ont pas voulu mourir, que se perdît par les sables leur torrent
    séminal.
Que j'écoute, dans la case enfumée que visite un reflet d'âmes
    propices

Ma tête sur ton sein chaud comme un dang au sortir du feu et
    fumant
20 Que je respire l'odeur de nos Morts, que je recueille et redise leur
    voix vivante, que j'apprenne à
Vivre avant de descendre, au delà du plongeur, dans les hautes
    profondeurs du sommeil.

Joal

Joal!
Je me rappelle.

Je me rappelle les signares à l'ombre verte des vérandas
Les signares aux yeux surréels comme un clair de lune sur la grève.

5 Je me rappelle les fastes du Couchant
Où Koumba N'Dofène voulait faire tailler son manteau royal.

Je me rappelle les festins funèbres fumant du sang des troupeaux
    égorgés
Du bruit des querelles, des rhapsodies des griots.

Je me rappelle les voix païennes rythmant le *Tantum Ergo*,
10 Et les processions et les palmes et les arcs de triomphe.

Je me rappelle la danse des filles nubiles
Les choeurs de lutte – oh! la danse finale des jeunes hommes, buste
Penché élancé, et le pur cri d'amour des femmes
– *Kor Siga!*

Je me rappelle, je me rapelle...
15 Ma tête rythmant
Quelle marche lasse le long des jours d'Europe où parfois
Apparaît un jazz orphelin qui sanglote sanglote sanglote.

Femme noire

Femme nue, femme noire
Vêtue de ta couleur qui est vie, de ta forme qui est beauté!
J'ai grandi à ton ombre; la douceur de tes mains bandait mes yeux.
Et voilà qu'au coeur de l'Eté et de Midi, je te découvre Terre promise,
    du haut d'un haut col calciné
5 Et ta beauté me foudroie en plein coeur, comme l'éclair d'un aigle.

Femme nue, femme obscure
Fruit mûr à la chair ferme, sombres extases du vin noir, bouche qui
    fais lyrique ma bouche
Savane aux horizons purs, savane qui frémis aux caresses ferventes du
    Vent d'Est
Tamtam sculpté, tamtam tendu qui grondes sous les doigts du
    Vainqueur
10 Ta voix grave de contre-alto est le chant spirituel de l'Aimée.

Femme nue, femme obscure
Huile que ne ride nul souffle, huile calme aux flancs de l'athlète, aux
    flancs des princes du Mali
Gazelle aux attaches célestes, les perles sont étoiles sur la nuit de ta
    peau
Délices des jeux de l'esprit, les reflets de l'or rouge sur ta peau qui se
    moire
15 A l'ombre de ta chevelure, s'éclaire mon angoisse aux soleils prochains
    de tes yeux.

Femme nue, femme noire
Je chante ta beauté qui passe, forme que je fixe dans l'Eternel,
Avant que le Destin jaloux ne te réduise en cendres pour nourrir les
    racines de la vie.

Neige sur Paris

Seigneur, vous avez visité Paris par ce jour de votre naissance
Parce qu'il devenait mesquin et mauvais
Vous l'avez purifié par le froid incorruptible
Par la mort blanche.
5 Ce matin, jusqu'aux cheminées d'usine qui chantent à l'unisson
Arborant des draps blancs
– 'Paix aux Hommes de bonne volonté!'

Seigneur, vous avez proposé la neige de votre Paix au monde divisé à
l'Europe divisée
A l'Espagne déchirée
10 Et le Rebelle juif et catholique a tiré ses 1400 canons contre les
montagnes de votre Paix.
Seigneur, j'ai accepté votre froid blanc qui brûle plus que le sel.
Voici que mon coeur fond comme neige sous le soleil.
J'oublie
Les mains blanches qui tirèrent les coups de fusils qui croulèrent les
empires
15 Les mains qui flagellèrent les esclaves, qui vous flagellèrent
Les mains blanches poudreuses qui vous giflèrent, les mains peintes
poudrées qui m'ont giflé
Les mains sûres qui m'ont livré à la solitude à la haine
Les mains blanches qui abattirent la forêt de rôniers qui dominait
l'Afrique, au centre de l'Afrique
Droits et durs, les Saras beaux comme les premiers hommes qui
sortirent de vos mains brunes.
20 Elles abattirent la forêt noire pour en faire des traverses de chemin de
fer
Elles abattirent les forêts d'Afrique pour sauver la Civilisation, parce
qu'on manquait de matière première humaine.

Seigneur, je ne sortirai pas ma réserve de haine, je le sais, pour les
diplomates qui montrent leurs canines longues
Et qui demain troqueront la chair noire.
Mon coeur, Seigneur, s'est fondu comme neige sur les toits de Paris
25 Au soleil de votre douceur.

Il est doux à mes ennemis, à mes frères aux mains blanches sans neige
A cause aussi des mains de rosée, le soir, le long de mes joues brûlantes.

Prière aux masques

Masques! O Masques!
Masque noir masque rouge, vous masques blanc-et-noir
Masques aux quatre points d'où souffle l'Esprit
Je vous salue dans le silence!
5 Et pas toi le dernier, Ancêtre à tête de lion
Vous gardez ce lieu forclos à tout rire de femme, à tout sourire qui se fane
Vous distillez cet air d'éternité où je respire l'air de mes Pères.
Masques aux visages sans masque, dépouillés de toute fossette comme de toute ride
Qui avez composé ce portrait, ce visage mien penché sur l'autel de papier blanc
10 A votre image, écoutez-moi!
Voici que meurt l'Afrique des empires – c'est l'agonie d'une princesse pitoyable
Et aussi l'Europe à qui nous sommes liés par le nombril.
Fixez vos yeux immuables sur vos enfants que l'on commande
Qui donnent leur vie comme le pauvre son dernier vêtement.
15 Que nous répondions présents à la renaissance du Monde
Ainsi le levain qui est nécessaire à la farine blanche.
Car qui apprendrait le rythme au monde défunt des machines et des canons?
Qui pousserait le cri de joie pour réveiller morts et orphelins à l'aurore?
Dites, qui rendrait la mémoire de vie à l'homme aux espoirs éventrés.
20 Ils nous disent les hommes du coton du café de l'huile
Ils nous disent les hommes de la mort.
Nous sommes les hommes de la danse, dont les pieds reprennent vigueur en frappant le sol dur.

Le totem

Il me faut le cacher au plus intime de mes veines
L'Ancêtre à la peau d'orage sillonnée d'éclairs et de foudre
Mon animal gardien, il me faut le cacher
Que je ne rompe le barrage des scandales.
5 Il est mon sang fidèle qui requiert fidélité
Protégeant mon orgueil nu contre
Moi-même et la superbe des races heureuses...

Que m'accompagnent kôras et balafong   *A René Maran*
(*Woï pour trois kôras et un balafong*)

I

Au détour du chemin la rivière, bleue par les prés frais de Septembre.
Un paradis que garde des fièvres une enfant aux yeux clairs comme
    deux épées
Paradis mon enfance africaine, qui gardait l'innocence de l'Europe.
Quels mois alors? Quelle année? Je me rappelle sa douceur fuyante
    au crépuscle
5 Que mouraient au loin les hommes comme aujourd'hui, que fraîche
    était, comme un limon, l'ombre des dakhârs.
Reposoirs opposés au bord de la plaine dure salée, de la grande voie
    étincelante des Esprits
Enclos méridien du côté des tombes!
Et toi Fontaine de Kam-Dyamé, quand à midi je buvais ton eau
    mystique au creux de mes mains
Entouré de mes compagnons lisses et nus et parés des fleurs de la
    brousse!
10 La flûte du pâtre modulait la lenteur des troupeaux
Et quand sur son ombre elle se taisait, résonnait le tamtam des tanns
    obsédés
Qui rythmait la théorie en fête des Morts.
Des tirailleurs jetaient leurs chéchias dans le cercle avec des cris
    aphones, et dansaient en flammes hautes mes soeurs
Téning-Ndyaré et Tyagoum-Ndyaré, plus claires maintenant que le
    cuivre d'outre-mer.

II

15 Fontaines plus tard, à l'ombre étroite des Muses latines que l'on
   proclamait mes anges protecteurs
   Puits de pierre, *Ngas-o-bil!* vous n'apaisâtes pas mes soifs.
   Mais après les pistaches grillées et salées, après l'ivresse des Vêpres et
   de midi
   Je me réfugiais vers toi, Fontaine-des-Eléphants à la bonne eau
   balbutiante
   Vers vous, mes Anciens, aux yeux graves qui approfondissent toutes
   choses.
20 Et me guidait par épines et signes Verdun oui Verdun, le chien qui
   gardait l'innocence de l'Europe.
   De tes rires de tes jeux de tes chansons, de tes fables qu'effeuille ma
   mémoire
   Je ne garde que le curé noir dansant
   Et sautant comme le Psalmiste devant l'Arche de Dieu, comme
   l'Ancêtre à la tête bien jointe
   Au rythme de nos mains: 'Ndyagâ-bâss! Ndyaga-rîti!'

III

25 *Entendez tambour qui bat!*
   Maman qui m'appelle.
   Elle m'a dit Toubab!
   D'embrasser la plus belle.
   Elle m'a dit 'Seigneur'!
30 Choisir! et délicieusement écartelé entre ces deux mains amies
   – Un baiser de toi Soukeîna! – ces deux mondes antagonistes
   Quand douloureusement – ah! je ne sais plus qui est ma soeur et qui
   ma soeur de lait
   De celles qui bercèrent mes nuits de leur tendresse rêvée, de leurs
   mains mêlées
   Quand douloureusement – un baiser de toi Isabelle! – entre ces deux
   mains
35 Que je voudrais unir dans ma main chaude de nouveau.
   Mais s'il faut choisir à l'heure de l'épreuve
   J'ai choisi le verset des fleuves, des vents et des forêts

L'assonance des plaines et des rivières, choisi le rythme de sang de
   mon corps dépouillé
Choisi la trémulsion des balafongs et l'accord des cordes et des cuivres
   qui semble faux, choisi le
40 Swing le swing oui le swing!
Et la lointaine trompette bouchée, comme une plainte de nébuleuse
   en dérive dans la nuit
Comme l'appel du Jugement, trompette éclatante sur les charniers
   neigeux d'Europe.
J'ai choisi mon peuple noir peinant, mon peuple paysan, toute la race
   paysanne par le monde.
'Et tes frères se sont irrités contre toi, ils t'ont mis à bêcher la terre.'
45 Pour être ta trompette!

IV

Mes agneaux, vous ma dilection avec ses yeux qui ne verront pas ma
   vieillesse
Je ne fus pas toujours pasteur de têtes blondes sur les plaines arides
   de vos livres
Pas toujours bon fonctionnaire, déférant envers ses supérieurs
Bon collègue poli élégant – et les gants? – souriant riant rarement
50 Vieille France vieille Université, et tout le chapelet déroulé.
Mon enfance, mes agneaux, est vieille comme le monde et je suis
   jeune comme l'aurore éternellement jeune du monde.
Les poétesses du sanctuaire m'ont nourri
Les griots du Roi m'ont chanté la légende véridique de ma race aux
   sons des hautes kôras.

V

Quels mois? quelle année?
55 Koumba Ndofène Dyouf régnait à Dyakhâw, superbe vassal
Et gouvernait l'administrateur du Sine-Saloum.
Le bruit de ses aïeux et des dyoung-dyoungs le précédait.
Le pèlerin royal parcourait ses provinces, écoutant dans le bois la
   complainte murmurée

Et les oiseaux qui babillaient, et le soleil sur leurs plumes était
    prodigue
60 Ecoutant la conque éloquente parmi les tombes sages.
Il appelait mon père 'Tokor'; ils échangeaient des énigmes que
    portaient des lévriers à grelots d'or
Pacifiques cousins, ils échangeaient des cadeaux sur les bords du
    Saloum
Des peaux précieuses des barres de sel, de l'or du Bouré de l'or du
    Boundou
Et de hauts conseils comme des chevaux du Fleuve.
65 L'Homme pleurait au soir, et dans l'ombre violette se lamentaient les
    khalams.

VI

J'étais moi-même le grand-père de mon grand-père
J'étais son âme et son ascendance, le chef de la maison d'Elissa du
    Gâbou
Droit dressé; en face, le Fouta-Djallong et l'Almamy du Fouta.
'On nous tue, Almamy! on ne nous déshonore pas.'
70 Ni ces montagnes ne purent nous dominer ni ses cavaliers nous
    encercler ni sa peau claire nous séduire
Ni nous abatardir ses prophètes.
Ma sève païenne est un vin vieux qui ne s'aigrit, pas le vin de palme
    d'un jour.
Et seize ans de guerre! seize ans le battement des tabalas du guerre
    des tabalas des balles!
Seize ans les nuages de poudre! seize ans de tornade sans un beau
    jour un seul
75 – Et chante vers les fontaines la théorie des jeunes filles aux seins
    triomphants comme des tours dans le soleil
Seize ans le crépuscule! et les femmes autour des sources étendent des
    pagnes rouges
Seize ans autour du marigot d'Elissa, que fleurissent les lances bruis-
    santes.
'On nous tue, Almamy!' Sur ce haut bûcher, j'air jeté
Toutes mes richesses poudreuses: mes trésors d'ambre gris et de
    cauris

30 Les captifs colonnes de ma maison, les épouses mères de mes fils
Les objets du sanctuaire, les masques graves et les robes solennelles
Mon parasol mon bâton de commandement, qui est de trois kintars
  d'ivoire
Et ma vieille peau.
Dormez, les héros, en ce soir accoucheur de vie, en cette nuit grave de
  grandeur.
35 Mais sauvée la Chantante, ma sève païenne qui monte et qui piaffe et
  qui danse
Mes deux filles aux chevilles délicates, les princesses cerclées de lourds
  bracelets de peine
Comme des paysannes. Des paysans les escortent pour être leurs
  seigneurs et leurs sujets
Et parmi elles, la mére de Sîra-Badral, fondatrice de royaumes
Qui sera le sel des Sérères, qui seront le sel des peuples salés.

VII

90 Elé-yâye! De nouveau je chante un noble sujet; que m'accompagnent
  kôras et balafong!
Princesse, pour toi ce chant d'or, plus haut que les abois des pédants!
Tu n'es pas plante parasite sur l'abondance rameuse de ton peuple.
Ils mentent; tu n'es pas tyran, tu ne te nourris pas de sa graisse.
Tu es l'organe riche de réserves, les greniers qui craquent pour les
  jours d'épreuve
95 – Ils nourrissent fourmis et colombes oisives.
Voilà, tu es, pour écarter au loin l'ennemi, debout, le tata
Je ne dis pas le silo, mais le chef qui organise la force qui forge
Le bras; mais la tête tata qui reçoit coups et boulets.
Et ton peuple s'honore en toi. Louange à ton peuple en toi!
00 Princesse de quatre coudées! au visage d'ombre autour de ta bouche
  de lumiére
Comme le soleil sur la plage de galets noirs
Tu es ton peuple.
La terre sombre de ta peau et féconde, généreusement il l'arrose de la
  tornade séminale.
Tu es son épouse, tu as reçu le sang sérère et le tribut de sang peul.
05 O sangs mêlés dans mes veines, seulement le battement nu des mains!

Que j'entende le choeur des voix vermeilles des sangs-mêlés!
Que j'entende le chant de l'Afrique future!

VIII

Ah! me soutient l'espoir qu'un jour je coure devant toi, Princesse,
    porteur de ta récade à l'assemblée des peuples.
C'est un cortège plus de grandeur que celui même de l'Empereur
    Gongo-Moussa en marche vers l'Orient étincelant.
110   O désert sans ombre désert, terre austère terre de pureté, de toutes
    mes petitesses
Lave-moi, de toutes mes contagions de civilisé.
Que me lave la face ta lumière qui n'est point subtile, que ta violence
    sèche me baigne dans une tornade de sable
Et tel le blanc méhari de race, que mes lèvres de neuf jours en neuf
    jours soient chastes de toute eau terrestre, et silencieuses.
Je marcherai par la terre nord-orientale, par l'Egypte des temples et
    des pyramides
115   Mais je vous laisse Pharaon qui m'a assis à sa droite et mon arrière-
    grand-père aux oreilles rouges.
Vos savants sauront prouver qu'ils étaient hyperboréens ainsi que
    toutes mes grandeurs ensevelies.
Cette colonne solennelle, ce ne sont plus quatre mille esclaves portant
    chacun cinq mithkals d'or
Ce sont sept mille nègres nouveaux, sept mille soldats sept mille
    paysans humbles et fiers
Qui portent les richesses de ma race sur leurs épaules musicales.
120   Ses richesses authentiques. Non plus l'or ni l'ambre ni l'ivoire, mais les
    produits d'authentiques paysans et de travailleurs à vingt centimes
    l'heure
Mais toutes les ruines pendant la traite européenne des nègres
Mais toutes les larmes par les trois continents, toutes les sueurs noires
    qui engraissèrent les champs de canne et de coton
Mais tous les hymnes chantés, toutes les mélopées déchirées par la
    trompette bouchée
Toutes les joies dansées oh! toute l'exultation criée.
125   Ce sont sept mille nègres nouveaux, sept mille soldats sept mille
    paysans humbles et fiers

Qui portent les richesses de ma race sur leurs épaules d'amphore
La Force la Noblesse la Candeur
Et comme d'une femme, l'abandonnement ravie à la grande force
  cosmique, à l'Amour qui meut les mondes chantants.

IX

Dans l'espoir de ce jour – voici que la Somme et la Seine et le Rhin et
  les sauvages fleuves slaves sont rouges sous l'épée de l'Archange
130 Et mon coeur va défaillant à l'odeur vineuse du sang, mais j'ai des
  consignes et le devoir de tenir
Qu'au moins me console, chaque soir, l'humeur voyageuse de mon
  double.
Tokô'Waly mon oncle, te souviens-tu des nuits de jadis quand
  s'appesantissait ma tête sur ton dos de patience?
Ou que me tenant par la main, ta main me guidait par ténèbres et
  signes?
Les champs sont fleurs de vers luisants; les étoiles se posent sur les
  herbes sur les arbres.
135 C'est le silence alentour.
Seuls bourdonnent les parfums de brousse, ruches d'abeilles rousses
  qui dominent la vibration grêle des grillons
Et tamtam voilé, la respiration au loin de la Nuit.
Toi Tokô'Waly, tu écoutes l'inaudible
Et tu m'expliques les signes que disent les Ancêtres dans la sérénité
  marine des constellations
140 La Taureau le Scorpion le Léopard, L'Eléphant les Poissons familiers
Et la pompe lactée des Esprits par le tann céleste qui ne finit point.
Mais voici l'intelligence de la déesse Lune et que tombent les voiles
  des ténébres.
Nuit d'Afrique ma nuit noire, mystique et claire noire et brillante
Tu reposes accordée à la terre, tu es la Terre et les collines har-
  monieuses.
145 O Beauté classique qui n'es point angle, mais ligne élastique élégante
  élancée!
O visage classique! depuis le front bombé sous la forêt de senteurs et
  les yeux larges obliques jusqu'à la baie gracieuse du menton et
L'élan fougueux des collines jumelles! O courbes de douceur visage
  mélodique!

O ma Lionne ma Beauté noire, ma Nuit noire ma Noire ma Nue!

Ah! que de fois as-tu fait battre mon coeur comme le léopard
    indompté dans sa cage étroite.

150 Nuit qui me délivres des raisons des salons des sophismes, des
    pirouettes des prétextes, des haines calculées des carnages human-
    isés

Nuit qui fonds toutes mes contradictions, toutes contradictions dans
    l'unité première de ta négritude

Reçois l'enfant toujours enfant, que douze ans d'errances n'ont pas
    vieilli.

Je n'amène d'Europe que cette enfant amie, la clarté de ses yeux
    parmi les brumes bretonnes.

Château-Gontier
Octobre–décembre 1939.

A l'appel de la race de Saba   *A Pierre Achille*
(*Woï pour deux kôras*)

Mère, sois bénie!

J'entends ta voix quand je suis livré au silence sournois de cette nuit
    d'Europe

Prisonnier de mes draps blancs et froids bien tirés, de toutes les
    angoisses qui m'embarrassent inextricablement

Quand fond sur moi, milan soudain, l'aigre panique des feuilles
    jaunes

5   Ou celle des guerriers noirs au tonnerre de la tornade des tanks

Et tombe leur chef avec un grand cri, dans une grande giration de
    tout le corps.

Mère, oh! j'entends ta voix courroucée.

Voilà tes yeux courroucés et rouges qui incendient nuit et brousse
    noire comme au jour jadis de mes fugues

– Je ne pouvais rester sourd à l'innocence des conques, des fontaines
    et des mirages sur les tanns

10 Et tremblait ton menton sous tes lèvres gonflées et tordues.

II

Mère, sois bénie!
Je me rappelle les jours de mes pères, les soirs de Dyilôr
Cette lumière d'outre-ciel des nuits sur la terre douce au soir.
Je suis sur les marches de la demeure profonde obscurément.
15 Mes frères et mes soeurs serrent contre mon coeur leur chaleur
     nombreuse de poussins.
Je repose la tête sur les genoux de ma nourrice Ngâ, de Ngâ la
     poétesse
Ma tête bourdonnant au galop guerrier des dyoung-dyoungs, au
     grand galop de mon sang de pur sang
Ma tête mélodieuse des chansons lointaines de Koumba l'Orpheline.
Au milieu de la cour, le ficus solitaire
20 Et devisent à son ombre lunaire les épouses de l'Homme de leurs voix
     graves et profondes comme leurs yeux et les fontaines nocturnes de
     Fimla.
Et mon père étendu sur des nattes paisibles, mais grand mais fort
     mais beau
Homme du Royaume de Sine, tandis qu'alentour sur les kôras, voix
     héroïques, les griots font danser leurs doigts du fougue
Tandis qu'au loin monte, houleuse de senteurs fortes et chaudes, la
     rumeur classique de cent troupeaux.

III

Mère, sois bénie!
25 Je ne souffle pas le vent d'Est sur ces images pieuses comme sur le
     sable des pistes
Tu ne m'entends pas quand je t'entends, telle la mère anxieuse qui
     oublie de presser le bouton du téléphone
Mais je n'efface les pas de mes pères ni des pères de mes pères dans
     ma tête ouverte à vents et pillards du Nord.
Mère, respire dans cette chambre peuplée de Latins et de Grecs
     l'odeur des victimes vespérales de mon coeur.
Qu'ils m'accordent, les génies protecteurs, que mon sang ne s'affadisse
     pas comme un assimilé comme un civilisé.

30 J'offre un poulet sans tache, debout près de l'Aîné, bien que tard
venu, afin qu'avant l'eau crémeuse et la bière de mil
Gicle jusqu'à moi et sur mes lèvres charnelles le sang chaud salé du
taureau dans la force de l'âge, dans la plénitude de sa graisse.

IV

Mère, sois bénie!
Nos aubes que saignent les jours proconsulaires deux générations
d'hommes et bien plus, n'ont-elles pas coloré tes yeux comme
solennellement les hautes herbes dans le carnage des hautes
flammes?
Mère, tu pleures le transfuge à l'heure de faiblesse qui précède le
sommeil, que l'on a verrouillé les portes et qu'aboient les chiens
jeunes aux Esprits
35 Depuis une neuvaine d'années; et moi ton fils, je médite je forge ma
bouche vaste retentissante pour l'écho et la trompette de libération
Dans l'ombre, Mère – mes yeux prématurément se sont faits
vieux – dans le silence et le brouillard sans odeur ni couleur
Comme le dernier forgeron. Ni maîtres désormais ni esclaves ni
guelwars ni griots de griot
Rien que la lisse et virile camaraderie des combats et que me soit égal
le fils du captif, que me soient copains le Maure et le Targui
congénitalement ennemis.
Car le cri montagnard du Ras Desta a traversé l'Afrique de part en
part, comme une épée longue et sûre dans l'avilissement de ses
reins.
40 Il a dominé la rage trépignante crépitante des mitrailleuses, défié les
avions des marchands
Et voici qu'un long gémissement, plus désolé qu'un long pleur de
mère aux funérailles d'un jeune homme
Sourd des mines là-bas, dans l'extrême Sud.

V

Mère, sois bénie!
J'ai vu – dans le sommeil léger de quelle aube gazouillée? – le jour de
libération.

45   C'était un jour pavoisé de lumière claquante, comme de drapeaux et
      d'oriflammes aux hautes couleurs.
      Nous étions là tous réunis, mes camarades les forts en thème et moi,
      tels aux premiers jours de guerre les nationaux débarqués de
      l'étranger
      Et mes premiers camarades de jeu, et d'autres et d'autres encore que
      je ne connaissais même pas de visage, que je reconnaissais à la
      fièvre de leur regard.
      Pour le dernier assaut contre les Conseils d'administration qui gouver-
      nent les gouverneurs des colonies.
      Comme aux dernières minutes avant l'attaque – les cartouchières sont
      bien garnies, le coup de pinard avalé; les musulmans ont du lait et
      tous les grigris de leur foi.
50   La mort nous attend peut-être sur la colline; la vie y pousse sur la
      mort dans le soleil chantant
      Et la victoire; sur la colline à l'air pur où les banquiers bedonnants ont
      bâti leurs villas, blanches et roses
      Loin des faubourgs, loin des misères des quartiers indigènes.

VI

      Mère, sois bénie!
      Reconnais ton fils parmi ses camarades comme autre-fois ton cham-
      pion. *Kor-Sanou!* parmi les athlètes antagonistes
55   A son nez fort et à la délicatesse de ses attaches.
      En avant! Et que ne soit pas le paean poussé ô Pindare! mais le cri de
      guerre hirsute et le coupe-coupe dégaîné
      Mais jaillie des cuivres de nos bouches, la Marseillaise de Valmy plus
      pressante que la charge d'éléphants des gros tanks que précèdent
      les ombres sanglantes
      La Marseillaise catholique.
      Car nous sommes là tous réunis, divers de teint – il y en a qui sont
      couleur de café grillé, d'autres bananes d'or et d'autres terre des
      rizières
60   Divers de traits de costume de coutumes de langue; mais au fond des
      yeux la même mélopée de souffrances à l'ombre des longs cils
      fiévreux
      Le Cafre le Kabyle le Somali le Maure, le Fân le Fôn le Bambara le
      Bobo le Mandiago

 IPS

Le nomade le mineur le prestataire, le paysan et l'artisan le boursier
et le tirailleur

Et tous les travailleurs blancs dans la lutte fraternelle.

Voici le mineur des Asturies le docker de Liverpool le Juif chassé
d'Allemagne, et Dupont et Dupuis et tous les gars de Saint-Denis.

VII

65 Mère, sois bénie!

Reconnais ton fils à l'authenticité de son regard, qui est celle de son
coeur et de son lignage

Reconnais ses camarades reconnais les combattants, et salue dans le
soir rouge de ta vieillesse

L'AUBE TRANSPARENTE D'UN JOUR NOUVEAU.   *Tours* 1936

Méditerranée

Et je redis ton nom: Dyallo!

Ta main et ma main quis'attarde; et nos pensées se cherchèrent dans
la mi-nuit de nos deux langues soeurs.

C'était en Méditerranée, nombril des races claires, bleue comme
jamais océan n'ont vu mes yeux

Qui souriait de ses millions de lèvres de lumière

5 Tandis que dix vaisseaux de ligne inflexible, telles des bouches
minces, bombardaient Almeria et qu'éclataient

Eclaboussant de sang de cervelle les murs noirs, comme des grenades,
des têtes ardentes d'enfants.

Nous parlions de l'Afrique.

Un vent tiède nous apportait son parfum plus chaud de femme noire

Ou celui que le vent souffle d'un champ de mil quand se heurtent les
épis lourds et que vole au-dessus une poussière or et brun.

10 Nous parlions du Fouta.

Noble était ton visage et d'ombre tes yeux et douces tes paroles
d'homme

Noble devait être ta race et bien née la femme de Timbo qui te
berçait le soir au rythme nocturne de la terre.

Et nous parlions du pays noir
Dans les cordages le soir, si près l'un de l'autre que nos épaules
    s'épousaient, fraternelles l'une à l'autre.
15 L'Afrique vivait là, au delà de l'oeil profane du jour, sous son visage
    noir étoilé
Dans les cales houleuses, saturées de la rumeur inquiète que menace
    la tornade.
Et s'échappaient, battements de tamtam, avec des éclats de rires ailés
    et des cris de cuivre dans deux cents langues
Des bouffées de vie dense que le vent dispersait dans l'air latin
Jusqu'au pont des premières où la jeune femme, libérée des sous-
    préfectures et de leurs rues étroites
20 Libérée des dernières mesures du tango et des bras de son danseur
Rêvait, au bord du mystère, de forêts aux senteurs viriles et d'espaces
    qui ignorent les fleurs...
Une grosse étoile montait, la dernière, éclairant ton front lisse quand
    nous nous quittâmes.
Et je redis ton nom: Dyallo!
Et tu redis mon nom: Senghor!   *Dakar* 1938

Luxembourg 1939

Ce matin du Luxembourg, cet automne du Luxembourg, comme je
    passais comme je repassais ma jeunesse
Sans flâneurs sans eaux, sans bateaux sur les eaux, sans enfants sans
    fleurs.
Ah! les fleurs de Septembre et les cris hâlés des enfants qui défiaient
    l'hiver prochain.
Seuls deux vieux gosses qui s'essayent à jouer au tennis.
5 Ce matin d'automne sans enfants – fermé le théâtre d'enfants!
Ce Luxembourg où je ne retrouve plus ma jeunesse, les années
    fraîches comme des pelouses.
Vaincus mes rêves désespérément mes camarades, se peut-il?
Les voici qui tombent comme les feuilles avec les feuilles, vieillis
    blessés à mort piétinés, tout sanglants de sang
Que l'on ramasse pour quelle fosse commune?
10 Je ne reconnais plus ce Luxembourg, ces soldats qui montent la
    garde.

On installe des canons pour protéger la retraite ruminante des
   Sénateurs
On creuse des tranchées sous le banc où j'appris la douceur éclose des
   lèvres.
Cet écriteau ah! oui, dangereuse jeunesse!...
Je vois tomber les feuilles dans les faux abris, dans les fosses dans les
   tranchées
15 Où ruisselle le sang d'une génération
L'Europe qui enterre le levain des nations et l'espoir des races
   nouvelles.

Camp 1940   *A Abdoulaye Ly*

Saccagé le jardin des fiançailles en un soir soudain de tornade
Fauchés les lilas blancs, fané le parfum des muguets
Parties les fiancées pour les Isles de brise et pour les Rivières du Sud.
Un cri de désastre a traversé de part en part le pays frais des vins et
   des chansons
5 Comme un glaive de foudre dans son coeur, du Levant au Ponant.

C'est un vaste village de boue et de branchages, un village crucifié par
   deux fosses de pestilences.
Haines et faim y fermentent dans la torpeur d'un été mortel.
C'est un grand village qu'encercle l'immobile hargne des barbelés
Un grand village sous la tyrannie de quatre mitrailleuses
   ombrageuses.
10 Et les nobles guerriers mendient des bouts de cigarette
Ils disputent les os aux chiens, ils se disputent chiens et chats de
   songe.
Mais seuls Ils ont gardé la candeur de leur rire, et seuls la liberté de
   leur âme de feu.
Et le soir tombe, sanglot de sang qui libère la nuit.
Ils veillent les grands enfants roses, leurs grands enfants blonds leurs
   grands enfants blancs
15 Qui se tournent et se retournent dans leur sommeil, hanté des puces
   du souci et des poux de captivité.
Les contes des veillées noires les bercent, et les voix graves qui
   épousent les sentiers du silence

Et les berceuses doucement, berceuses sans tamtam et sans battements
    de mains noires
– Ce sera pour demain, à l'heure de la sieste, le mirage des épopées
Et la chevauchée du soleil sur les savanes blanches aux sables sans
    limites.

20 Et le vent est guitare dans les arbres, les barbelés sont plus mélodieux
    que les cordes des harpes
Et les toits se penchent écoutent, les étoiles sourient de leurs yeux
    sans sommeil
– Là-haut là-haut, leur visage est bleu-noir.
L'air se fait tendre au village de boue et de branchages
Et la terre se fait humaine comme les sentinelles, les chemins les
    invitent à la liberté.

25 Ils ne partiront pas. Ils ne déserteront les corvées ni leur devoir de
    joie.
Qui fera les travaux de honte si ce n'est ceux qui sont nés nobles?
Qui donc dansera le dimanche aux sons du tamtam des gamelles?
Et ne sont-ils pas libres de la liberté du destin?

Saccagé le jardin des fiançailles en un soir soudain de tornade
30 Fauchés les lilas blancs, fané le parfum des muguets
Parties les fiancées pour les Isles de brise et pour les Rivières du Sud.

Front-Stalag 230

Taga de Mbaye Dyôb
(*pour un tama*)

Mbaye Dyôb! je veux dire ton nom et ton honneur.

Dyôb! je veux hisser ton nom au haut mât du retour, sonner ton nom
    comme la cloche qui chante la victoire
Je veux chanter ton nom Dyôbène! toi qui m'appelais ton maître et
Me réchauffais de ta ferveur aux soirs d'hiver autour du poêle rouge
    qui donnait froid.
5 Dyôb! qui ne sais remonter ta généalogie et domestiquer le temps
    noir, dont les ancêtres ne sont pas rythmés par la voix du tama
Toi qui n'as tué un lapin, qui t'es terré sous les bombes des grands
    vautours

Dyôb! – qui n'es ni capitaine ni aviateur ni cavalier pétaradant, pas
seulement du train des équipages
Mais soldat de deuxième classe au Quatrième Régiment des Tirailleurs sénégalais
Dyôb! – je veux chanter ton honneur blanc.

10   Les vierges du Gandyol te feront un arc de triomphe de leurs bras
courbes, de leurs bras d'argent et d'or rouge
Te feront une voie de gloire avec leurs pagnes rares des Rivières du
Sud.
Lors elles te feront un collier d'ivoire de leurs bouches qui parent plus
que manteau royal
Lors elles berceront ta marche, leurs voix se mêleront aux vagues de
la mer
Lors elles chanteront: 'Tu as bravé plus que la mort, plus que les
tanks et les avions qui sont rebelles aux sortilèges
15   Tu as bravé la faim, tu as bravé le froid et l'humiliation du captif.
Oh! téméraire, tu as été le marche-pied des griots des bouffons
Oh! toi qui ajoutas quels clous à ton calcaire pour ne pas déserter tes
compagnons
Pour ne pas rompre le pacte tacite
Pour ne pas laisser ton fardeau aux camarades, dont les dos ploient à
tout départ
20   Dont les bras s'alanguissent chaque soir où l'on serre une main de
moins
Et le front devient plus noir d'être éclairé par un regard de moins
Les yeux s'enfoncent quand s'y reflète un sourire de moins.'
Dyôb! – du Ngâbou au Wâlo, du Ngalam à la Mer s'élèveront les
chants des vierges d'ambre
Et que les accompagnent les cordes des kôras! Et que les accompagnent les vagues et les vents!
25   Dyôb! – je dis ton nom et ton honneur.   *Front-Stalag 230*

Ndessé

Mère, on m'écrit que tu blanchis comme la brousse à l'extrême
    hivernage
Quand je devais être ta fête, la fête gymnique de tes moissons
Ta saison belle avec sept fois neuf ans sans nuages et les greniers
    pleins à craquer de fin mil
Ton champion *Kor-Sanou!* Tel le palmier de Katamague
5   Il domine tous ses rivaux de sa tête au mouvant panache d'argent
Et les cheveux des femmes s'agitent sur leurs épaules, et les coeurs
    des vierges dans le tumulte de leur poitrine.

Voici que je suis devant toi Mère, soldat aux manches nues
Et je suis vêtu de mots étrangers, où tes yeux ne voient qu'un
    assemblage de bâtons et de haillons.
Si je te pouvais parler Mère! Mais tu n'entendrais qu'un gazouillis
    précieux et tu n'entendrais pas
10   Comme lorsque, bonnes femmes de sérères, vous déridiez le dieu aux
    troupeaux de nuages
Pétaradant des coups de fusil par-dessus le cliquetis des mots *para
gnessés.*
Mère, parle-moi. Ma langue glisse sur nos mots sonores et durs.
Tu les sais faire doux et moelleux comme à ton fils chéri autrefois.
Ah! me pèse le fardeau pieux de mon mensonge
15   Je ne suis plus le fonctionnaire qui a autorité, le marabout aux
    disciples charmés.
L'Europe m'a broyé comme le plat guerrier sous les pattes
    pachydermes des tanks
Mon coeur est plus meurtri que mon corps jadis, au retour des
    lointaines escapades aux bords enchantés des Esprits.

Je devais être, Mère, le palmier florissant de ta vieillesse, je te
    voudrais rendre l'ivresse de tes jeunes années.
Je ne suis plus que ton enfant endolori, et il se tourne et retourne sur
    ses flancs douloureux
20   Je ne suis plus qu'un enfant qui se souvient de ton sein maternel et
    qui pleure.
Reçois-moi dans la nuit qu'éclaire l'assurance de ton regard

Redis-moi les vieux contes des veillées noires, que je me perde par les
  routes sans mémoire.
Mére, je suis un soldat humilié qu'on nourrit de gros mil.

Dis-moi donc l'orgueil de mes pères!   *Front-Stalag* 230

Lettre à un prisonnier

Ngom! champion de Tyâné!

C'est moi qui te salue, moi ton voisin de village et de coeur.
Je te lance mon salut blanc comme le cri blanc de l'aurore, par-dessus
  les barbelés
De la haine et de la sottise, et je te nomme par ton nom et ton
  honneur.
5   Mon salut au Tamsir Dargui Ndyâye qui se nourrit de parchemins
Qui lui font la langue subtile et les doigts plus fins et plus longs
A Samba Dyouma le poète, et sa voix est couleur de flamme, et son
  front porte les marques du destin
A Nyaoutt Mbodye, à Koli Ngom ton frère de nom
A tous ceux qui, à l'heure où les grands bras sont tristes comme des
  branches battues de soleil
10   Le soir, se groupent frissonnants autour du plat de l'amitié.

Je t'écris dans la solitude de ma résidence surveillée – et chère – de ma
  peau noire.
Heureux amis, qui ignorez les murs de glace et les appartements trop
  clairs qui stérilisent
Toute graine sur les masques d'ancêtres et les souvenirs mêmes de
  l'amour.
Vous ignorez le bon pain blanc et le lait et le sel, et les mets
  substantiels qui ne nourrissent pas, qui divisent les civils
15   Et la foule des boulevards, les somnambules qui ont renié leur identité
  d'homme
Caméléons sourds de la métamorphose, et leur honte vous fixe dans
  votre cage de solitude.

Vous ignorez les restaurants et les piscines, et la noblesse au sang noir
    interdite
Et la Science et l'Humanité, dressant leurs cordons de police aux
    frontières de la négritude.
Faut-il crier plus fort? ou m'entendez-vous, dites?
20   Je ne reconnais plus les hommes blancs, mes frères
Comme ce soir au cinéma, perdus qu'ils étaient au delà du vide fait
    autour de ma peau.

Je t'écris parce que mes livres sont blancs comme l'ennui, comme la
    misère et comme la mort.
Faites-moi place autour du poêle, que je reprenne ma place encore
    tiède.
Que nos mains se touchent en puisant dans le riz fumant de l'amitié
25   Que les vieux mots sérères de bouche en bouche passent comme une
    pipe amicale.
Que Dargui nous partage ses fruits succulents – foin de toute
    sécheresse parfumée!
Toi, sers-nous tes bons mots, énormes comme le nombril de l'Afrique
    prodigieuse.
Quel chanteur ce soir convoquera tous les Ancêtres autour de nous
Autour de nous le troupeau pacifique des bêtes de la brousse?
30   Qui logera nos rêves sous les paupières des étoiles?

Ngom! réponds-moi par le courrier de la lune nouvelle.
Au détour du chemin, j'irai au devant de tes mots nus qui hésitent.
    C'est l'oiselet au sortir de sa cage
Tes mots si naïvement assemblés; et les doctes en rient, et ils me
    restituent le surréel
Et le lait m'en rejaillit au visage.
35   J'attends ta lettre à l'heure où le matin terrasse la mort noire.
Je la recevrai pieusement comme l'ablution matinale, comme la rosée
    de l'aurore.   *Paris, Juin* 1942

Chant de printemps   *Pour une jeune fille noire au talon rose*

Des chants d'oiseaux montent lavés dans le ciel primitif
L'odeur verte de l'herbe monte, Avril!
J'entends le souffle de l'aurore émouvant les nuages blancs de mes
    rideaux
J'entends la chanson du soleil sur mes volets mélodieux
5   Je sens comme une haleine et le souvenir de Naëtt sur ma nuque nue
    qui s'émeut
Et mon sang complice malgré moi chuchote dans mes veines.
C'est toi mon amie – ô! écoute les souffles déjà chauds dans l'avril d'un
    autre continent
Oh! écoute quand glissent glacées d'azur les ailes des hirondelles
    migratrices
Ecoute le bruissement blanc et noir des cigognes à l'extrême de leurs
    voiles déployées
10 Ecoute le message du printemps d'un autre âge d'un autre continent
Ecoute le message de l'Afrique lointaine et le chant de ton sang!
J'écoute la sève d'Avril qui dans tes veines chante.

II

Tu m'as dit:
– Ecoute mon ami, lointain et sourd, le grondement précoce de la
    tornade comme un feu roulant de brousse
15 Et mon sang crie d'angoisse dans l'abandon de ma tête trop lourde
    livrée aux courants électriques.
Ah! là-bas l'orage soudain, c'est l'incendie des côtes blanches, de la
    blanche paix de l'Afrique mienne.
Et dans la nuit où tonnent de grandes déchirures de métal
Entends plus près de nous, sur trois cents kilomètres, tous les hurle-
    ments des chacals sans lune et les miaulements félins des balles
Entends les rugissements brefs des canons et les barrissements des
    pachydermes de cent tonnes.
20 Est-ce l'Afrique encore cette côte mouvante, cet ordre de bataille, cette
    longue ligne rectiligne, cette ligne d'acier et de feu?....
Mais entends l'ouragan des aigles-forteresses, les escadres aériennes
    tirant à pleins sabords

Et foudroyant les capitales dans la seconde de l'éclair.
Et les lourdes locomotives bondissent au-dessus des cathédrales
Et les cités superbes flambent, mais bien plus jaunes mais bien plus
    sèches qu'herbes de brousse en saison sèche.
25   Et voici que les hautes tours, orgueil des hommes, tombent comme les
    géants des forêts avec un bruit de platras
Et voici que les édifices de ciment et d'acier fondent comme la cire
    molle aux pieds de Dieu.
Et le sang de mes frères blancs bouillonne par les rues, plus rouge
    que le Nil – sous quelle colère de Dieu?
Et le sang de mes frères noirs les Tirailleurs sénégalais, dont chaque
    goutte répandue est une pointe de feu à mon flanc.
Printemps tragique! Printemps de sang! Est-ce là ton message,
    Afrique?...
30   Oh! mon ami – ô! comment entendrai-je ta voix? Comment voir ton
    visage noir si doux à ma joue brune à ma joie brune
Quand il faut me boucher les yeux et les oreilles?

III

Je t'ai dit:
– Ecoute le silence sous les colères flamboyantes de l'orage
La voix de l'Afrique planant au-dessus de la rage des canons longs
35   La voix de ton coeur de ton sang, écoute-la sous le délire de la tête de
    tes cris.
Est-ce sa faute si Dieu lui a demandé les prémices de ses moissons
Les plus beaux épis et les plus beaux corps élus patiemment parmi
    mille peuples?
Est-ce sa faute si Dieu fait de ses fils les verges à châtier la superbe
    des nations?
Ecoute sa voix bleue dans l'air lavé de haine, vois le sacrificateur
    verser les libations au pied du tumulus.
40   Elle proclame le grand émoi qui fait trembler les corps aux souffles
    chauds d'Avril
Elle proclame l'attente amoureuse du renouveau dans la fièvre de ce
    printemps
La vie qui fait vagir deux enfants nouveau-nés au bord d'un tombeau
    cave.

Elle dit ton baiser plus fort que la haine et la mort.
Je vois au fond de tes yeux troubles la lumière étale de l'Eté
45 Je respire entre tes collines l'ivresse douce des moissons.
Ah! cette rosée de lumière aux ailes frémissantes de tes narines!
Et ta bouche est comme un bourgeon qui se gonfle au soleil
Et comme une rose couleur de vin vieux qui va s'épanouir au chant
    de tes lévres.
Ecoute le message, mon amie sombre au talon rose.
50 J'entends ton coeur d'ambre qui germe dans le silence et le
    Printemps.   *Paris, Avril* 1944

Prière de paix   *A Georges et Claude Pompidou*
(*pour grandes orgues*)
'Sicut et nos dimittimus debitoribus nostris'

I

Seigneur Jésus, à la fin de ce livre que je T'offre comme un ciboire de
    souffrances
Au commencement de la Grande Année, au soleil de Ta paix sur les
    toits neigeux de Paris
– Mais je sais bien que le sang de mes frères rougira de nouveau
    l'Orient jaune, sur les bords de l'Océan Pacifique que violent
    tempêtes et haines
Je sais bien que ce sang est la libation printanière dont les Grands-
    Publicains depuis septante années engraissent les terres d'Empire
5 Seigneur, au pied de cette croix – et ce n'est plus Toi l'arbre de
    douleur, mais au-dessus de l'Ancien et du Nouveau Monde
    l'Afrique crucifiée
Et son bras droit s'étend sur mon pays, et son côté gauche ombre
    l'Amérique
Et son coeur est Haïti cher, Haïti qui osa proclamer l'Homme en face
    du Tyran
Au pied de mon Afrique crucifiée depuis quatre cents ans et pourtant
    respirante
Laisse-moi Te dire Seigneur, sa prière de paix et de pardon.

II

10 Seigneur Dieu, pardonne à l'Europe blanche!
Et il est vrai, Seigneur, que pendant quatre siècles de lumières, elle a jeté la bave et les abois de ses molosses sur mes terres
Et les chrétiens, abjurant Ta lumière et la mansuétude de Ton coeur
Ont éclairé leurs bivouacs avec mes parchemins, torturé mes talbés, déporté mes docteurs et mes maîtres-de-science.
Leur poudre a croulé dans l'éclair la fierté des tatas et des collines
15 Et leurs boulets ont traversé les reins d'empires vastes comme le jour clair, de la Corne de l'Occident jusqu'à l'Horizon oriental
Et comme des terrains de chasse, ils ont incendié les bois intangibles, tirant Ancêtres et génies par leur barbe paisible.
Et ils ont fait de leur mystère la distraction dominicale de bourgeois somnambules.
Seigneur, pardonne à ceux qui ont fait des Askia des maquisards, de mes princes des adjudants
De mes domestiques des boys et de mes paysans des salariés, de mon peuple un peuple de prolétaires.
20 Car il faut bien que Tu pardonnes à ceux qui ont donné la chasse à mes enfants comme à des éléphants sauvages.
Et ils les ont dressés à coups de chicotte, et ils ont fait d'eux les mains noires de ceux dont les mains étaient blanches.
Car il faut bien que Tu oublies ceux qui ont exporté dix millions de mes fils dans les maladreries de leurs navires
Qui en ont supprimé deux cents millions.
Et ils m'ont fait une vieillesse solitaire parmi la forêt de mes nuits et la savane de mes jours.
25 Seigneur la glace de mes yeux s'embue
Et voilà que le serpent de la haine lève la tête dans mon coeur, ce serpent que j'avais cru mort...

III

Tue-le Seigneur, car il me faut poursuivre mon chemin, et je veux prier singulièrement pour la France.
Seigneur, parmi les nations blanches, place la France à la droite du Père.

Oh! je sais bien qu'elle aussi est l'Europe, qu'elle m'a ravi mes enfants
comme un brigand du Nord des boeufs, pour engraisser ses terres à
cannes et coton, car la sueur nègre est fumier.

30   Qu'elle aussi a porté la mort et le canon dans mes villages bleus,
qu'elle a dressé les miens les uns contre les autres comme des chiens
se disputant un os

Qu'elle a traité les résistants de bandits, et craché sur les têtes-aux-
vastes-desseins.

Oui Seigneur, pardonne à la France qui dit bien la voie droite et
chemine par les sentiers obliques

Qui m'invite à sa table et me dit d'apporter mon pain, qui me donne
de la main droite et de la main gauche enlève la moitié.

Oui Seigneur, pardonne à la France qui hait les occupants et
m'impose l'occupation si gravement

35   Qui ouvre des voies triomphales aux héros et traite ses Sénégalais en
mercenaires, faisant d'eux les dogues noirs de l'Empire

Qui est la République et livre les pays aux Grands-Concessionnaires

Et de ma Mésopotamie, de mon Congo, ils ont fait un grand cimetière
sous le soleil blanc.

IV

Ah! Seigneur, éloigne de ma mémoire la France qui n'est pas la
France, ce masque de petitesse et de haine sur le visage de la
France

Ce masque de petitesse et de haine pour qui je n'ai que haine – mais
je peux bien haïr le Mal

40   Car j'ai une grande faiblesse pour la France.

Bénis ce peuple garrotté qui par deux fois sut libérer ses mains et osa
proclamer l'avènement des pauvres à la royauté

Qui fit des esclaves du jour des hommes libres égaux fraternels

Bénis ce peuple qui m'a apporté Ta Bonne Nouvelle, Seigneur, et
ouvert mes paupières lourdes à la lumière de la foi.

Il a ouvert mon coeur à la connaissance du monde, me montrant
l'arc-en-ciel des visages neufs de mes frères.

45   Je vous salue mes frères: toi Mohamed Ben Abdallah, toi
Razafymahatrata, et puis toi là-bas Pham-Manh-Tuong, vous des
mers pacifiques et vous des forêts enchantées

Je vous salue tous d'un coeur catholique.

Ah! je sais bien que plus d'un de Tes messagers a traqué mes prêtres comme gibier et fait un grand carnage d'images pieuses.

Et pourtant on aurait pu s'arranger, car elles furent, ces images, de la terre à Ton ciel l'échelle de Jacob

La lampe au beurre clair qui permet d'attendre l'aube, les étoiles qui préfigurent le soleil.

50 Je sais que nombre de Tes missionnaires ont béni les armes de la violence et pactisé avec l'or des banquiers

Mais il faut qu'il y ait des traîtres et des imbéciles.

V

O bénis ce peuple, Seigneur, qui cherche son propre visage sous le masque et a peine à le reconnaître

Qui Te cherche parmi le froid, parmi la faim qui lui rongent os et entrailles

Et la fiancée pleure sa viduité, et le jeune homme voit sa jeunesse cambriolée

55 Et la femme lamente oh! l'oeil absent de son mari, et la mère cherche le rêve de son enfant dans les gravats.

O bénis ce peuple qui rompt ses liens, bénis ce peuple aux abois qui fait front à la meute boulimique des puissants et des tortionnaires.

Et avec lui tous les peuples d'Europe, tous les peuples d'Asie tous les peuples d'Afrique et tous les peuples d'Amérique

Qui suent sang et souffrances. Et au milieu de ces millions de vagues, vois les têtes houleuses de mon peuple.

Et donne à leurs mains chaudes qu'elles enlacent la terre d'une ceinture de mains fraternelles

60 DESSOUS L'ARC-EN-CIEL DE TA PAIX.   *Paris, Janvier* 1945

Congo

(woï pour trois kôras et un balafong)

Oho! Congo oho! Pour rythmer ton nom grand sur les eaux sur les
fleuves sur toute mémoire
Que j'émeuve la voix des kôras Koyaté! L'encre du scribe est sans
mémoire.

Oho! Congo couchée dans ton lit de forêts, reine sur l'Afrique
domptée
Que les phallus des monts portent haut ton pavillon
5 Car tu es femme par ma tête par ma langue, car tu es femme par
mon ventre
Mère de toutes choses qui ont narines, des crocodiles des hippopotames
Lamantins iguanes poissons oiseaux, mère des crues nourrice des
moissons.
Femme grande! eau tant ouverte à la rame et à l'étrave des pirogues
Ma Saô mon amante aux cuisses furieuses, aux longs bras de
nénuphars calmes
10 Femme précieuse d'ouzougou, corps d'huile imputrescible à la peau
de nuit diamantine.
Toi calme Déesse au sourire étale sur l'élan vertigineux de ton sang
O toi l'Impaludée de ton lignage, délivre-moi de la surrection de mon
sang.
Tam-Tam toi toi tam-tam des bonds de la panthère, de la stratégie
des fourmis
Des haines visqueuses au jour troisième surgies du potopoto des
marais
15 Hâ! sur toute chose, du sol spongieux et des chants savonneux de
l'Homme-blanc
Mais délivre-moi de la nuit sans joie, et guette le silence des foréts.
Donc que je sois le fût splendide et le bond de vingt-six coudées
Dans l'alizé, sois la fuite de la pirogue sur l'élan lisse de ton ventre.
Clairières de ton sein îles d'amour, collines d'ambre et de gongo
20 Tanns d'enfance tanns de Joal, et ceux de Dyilôr en Septembre
Nuits d'Ermenonville en Automne – il avait fait trop beau trop doux.
Fleurs sereines de tes cheveux, pétales si blancs de ta bouche
Surtout les doux propos à la néoménie, jusques à la mi-nuit du sang.
Délivre-mois de la nuit de mon sang, car guette le silence des forêts.

25 Mon amante à mon flanc, dont l'huile fait docile mes mains mon âme
    Ma force s'érige dans l'abandon, mon honneur dans la soumission
    Et ma science dans l'instinct de ton rythme. Noue son élan le
        coryphée
    A la proue de son sexe, comme le fier chasseur de lamantins.
    Rythmez clochettes rythmez langues rythmez rames la danse du
        Maître des rames.
30 Ah! elle est digne, sa pirogue, des choeurs triomphants de Fadyoutt
    Et je clame deux fois deux mains de tam-tams, quarante vierges à
        chanter ses gestes.
    Rythmez la flèche rutilante, la griffe à midi du Soleil
    Rythmez, crécelles des cauris, les bruissements des Grandes Eaux
    Et la mort sur la crête de l'exultation, à l'appel irrécusable du gouffre.

35 Mais la pirogue renaîtra par les nénuphars de l'écume
    Surnagera la douceur des bambous au matin transparent du monde.

Le Kaya-Magan

(*woï pour kôra*)

KAYA-MAGAN je suis! la personne première
Roi de la nuit noire de la nuit d'argent, Roi de la nuit de verre.
Paissez mes antilopes à l'abri des lions, distants au charme de ma voix.
Le ravissement de vous émaillant les plaines du silence!
5 Vous voici quotidiennes mes fleurs mes étoiles, vous voici à la joie de
       mon festin.
Donc paissez mes mamelles d'abondance, et je ne mange pas qui suis
       source de joie
Paissez mes seins forts d'homme, l'herbe de lait qui luit sur ma .
       poitrine.

Que l'on allume chaque soir douze mille étoiles sur la Grand-Place
Que l'on chauffe douze mille écuelles cerclées du serpent de la mer
       pour mes sujets
10 Très pieux, pour les faons de mon flanc, les résidents de ma maison
       et leurs clients
Les Guélowars des neuf tatas et les villages des brousses barbares

Pour tous ceux-là qui sont entrés par les quatre portes sculptées – la
   marche
Solennelle de mes peuples patients! leurs pas se perdent dans les
   sables de l'Histoire.
Pour les blancs du Septentrion, les nègres du Midi d'un bleu si doux.
15 Et je ne dénombre les rouges du Ponant, et pas les transhumants du
   Fleuve!
Mangez et dormez enfants de ma sève, et vivez votre vie des grandes
   profondeurs
Et paix sur vous qui déclinez. Vous respirez par mes narines.

Je dis KAYA-MAGAN je suis! Roi de la lune, j'unis la nuit et le jour
Je suis Prince du Nord du Sud, du Soleil-levant Prince et du Soleil-
   couchant
20 La plaine ouverte à mille ruts, la matrice où se fondent les métaux
   précieux.
Il en sort l'or rouge et l'Homme rouge-rouge ma dilection à moi
Le Roi de l'or – qui a la splendeur du midi, la douceur féminine de la
   nuit.
Donc picorez mon front bombé, oiseaux de mes cheveux serpents.
Vous ne vous nourrissez seulement de lait bis, mais picorez la cervelle
   du Sage
25 Maître de l'hiéroglyphe dans sa tour de verre.

Paissez faons de mon flanc sous ma récade et mon croissant de lune.
Je suis le Buffle qui se rit du Lion, de ses fusils chargés jusqu'à la
   gueule.
Et il faudra bien qu'il se prémunisse dans l'enceinte de ses murailles.
Mon empire est celui des proscrits de César, des grands bannis de la
   raison ou de l'instinct
30 Mon empire est celui d'Amour, et j'ai faiblesse pour toi femme
L'Etrangère aux yeux de clairière, aux lèvres de pomme cannelle au
   sexe de buisson ardent
Car je suis les deux battants de la porte, rythme binaire de l'espace, et
   le troisième temps
Car je suis le mouvement du tam-tam, force de l'Afrique future.
Dormez faons de mon flanc sous mon croissant de lune.

L'Absente

(*woï pour trois kôras et un balafong*)

Jeunes filles aux gorges vertes, plus ne chantez votre Champion et
    plus ne chantez l'Elancé.
Mais je ne suis pas votre honneur, pas le Lion téméraire, le Lion vert
    qui rugit l'honneur du Sénégal.
Ma tête n'est pas d'or, elle ne vêt pas de hauts desseins
Sans bracelets pesants sont mes bras que voilà, mes mains si nues!
5   Je ne suis pas le Conducteur. Jamais tracé sillon ni dogme comme le
    Fondateur
La ville aux quatre portes, jamais proféré mot à graver sur la pierre.
Je dis bien: je suis le Dyâli.

II

Jeunes filles aux longs cous de roseaux, je dis chantez l'Absente la
    Princesse en allée.
Ma gloire n'est pas sur la stèle, ma gloire n'est pas sur la pierre
10 Ma gloire est de chanter le charme de l'Absente
Ma gloire de charmer le charme de l'Absente, ma gloire
Est de chanter la mousse et l'élyme des sables
La poussière des vagues et le ventre des mouettes, la lumière sur les
    collines
Toutes choses vaines sous le van, toutes choses vaines dans le vent et
    l'odeur des charniers
15 Toutes choses frêles dans la lumière des armes, toutes choses très
    belles dans la spendeur des armes
Ma gloire est de chanter la beauté de l'Absente.

III

Or c'était une nuit d'hiver lorsque dehors mûrit le gel, que les deux
    corps sont fraternels.
Les sifflets des rapides traversaient mon coeur longuement, de longs
    déchirements de pointes de diamant.
J'ai réveillé les concubines alentour.

20 Ah! ce sommeil sourd qui irrite quand chaque flanc et le dos sont les
plaies du crucifié.
La poitrine succombe à de graves énigmes, et je meurs de ne pas
mourir et je meurs de vivre le coeur absent.
Elles m'ont parlé de l'Absente doucement
Doucement elles m'ont chanté dans l'ombre le chant de l'Absente,
comme on berce le beau bébé de sa chair brune
Mais qu'elle reviendrait la Reine de Saba à l'annonce des flamboyants.
25 De très loin la Bonne Nouvelle est annoncée par les collines, sur les
pistes ferventes par les chameliers au long cours.
Dites! qu'elle est longue à mon coeur l'absence de l'Absente.

IV

Jeunes filles aux seins debout, chantez la sève annoncez le Printemps.
Une goutte d'eau n'est tombée depuis six mois, pas un mot tendre et
pas un bourgeon à sourire.
Rien que l'aigreur de l'Harmattan, comme les dents du trigonocéphale
30 Au mieux rien qu'un soulèvement de sables, rien qu'un tourbillon de
pruine et de pailles et de balles et d'ailes et d'élytres
Des choses mortes sous l'aigre érosion de la raison.
Rien que le Vent d'Est dans nos gorges plus que citernes au désert
Vides. Mais cette rumeur dans nos jambes, ce surgissement de la sève
Qui gonfle les bourgeons à l'aine des jeunes hommes, réveille les
huîtres perlières sous les palétuviers...
35 Ecoutez jeunes filles le chant de la sève qui monte à vos gorges
debout.
Vert et vert le Printemps au clair mitan de Mai, d'un vert si tendre
ho! que c'est ravissement.
Ce n'est pas la floraison flave des cassias, les étoiles splendides des
cochlospermums
Sur le sol de ténèbres, l'intelligence du Soleil ô Circonsis!
C'est la tendresse du vert par l'or des savanes, vert et or couleurs de
l'Absente
40 C'est la surrection de la sève jusqu'à la nuque debout qui s'émeut.

V

Sa venue nous était prédite quand les palabres rougiraient les places
  des villages, les boutiques des bidonvilles et les ateliers des manufac-
  tures.
Je sais que les épouses émigrent déjà chez leur mère; les jeunes gens
  arrachent aux lamarques leur part de l'indivis
Les biens publics sont vendus à l'encan, les Grands organisent leurs
  femmes en pool charbon-acier
Des tentes pourpres sont dressées aux carrefours, avec des rues
  barrées et sens uniques.
45 Luxe et licence!...Sa venue nous était prédite quand se rassem-
  bleraient les hirondelles. Voilà
Qu'à tire-d'aile elles fuient les chaleurs de nos querelles intestines.
Puisque reverdissent nos jambes pour la danse de la moisson
Je sais qu'elle viendra la Très Bonne Nouvelle
Au solstice de Juin, comme dans l'an de la défaite et dans l'an de
  l'espoir.
50 La précèdent de longs mirages de dromadaires, graves des essences
  de sa beauté.
La voilà l'Ethiopienne, fauve comme l'or mûr incorruptible comme
  l'or
Douce d'olive, bleu souriante de son visage fin souriante dans sa
  prestance
Vêtue de vert et de nuage. Parée du pentagramme.

VI

Salut de son féal à la Souriante et louange loyale.
55 Kôriste de sa cour et dément de son charme!...Ma gloire n'est pas
  sur la stèle
Ni ma voix ne sera sur pierre pétrifiée, mais voix rythmée d'une voix
  juste.
Qu'elle germe dans la mémoire de l'Absente qui règne sur mes
  horizons de verre
Mûrisse dans la vôtre ô jeunes filles, comme la farine futile pour
  nourrir tout un peuple.

Donc je nommerai les choses futiles qui fleuriront de ma
  nomination – mais le nom de l'Absente est ineffable.
60 Ses mains d'alizés qui guérissent des fièvres
  Ses paupières de fourrure et de pétales de laurier-rose
  Ses cils ses sourcils secrets et purs comme des hiéroglyphes
  Ses cheveux bruissants comme un feu roulant de brousse la nuit.
  Tes yeux ta bouche hâ! ton secret qui monte à la nuque...
65 Des choses vaines. Ce n'est pas le savoir qui nourrit ton peuple
  Ce sont les mets que tu leur sers par les mains du kôriste et par la
  voix.
  Woï! donc salut à la Souriante qui donne le souffle à mes narines, qui
  coupe le souffle à mes narines et engorge ma gorge
  Salut à la Présente qui me fascine par le regard noir du mamba, tout
  constellé d'or et de vert
  Et je suis colombe-serpent, et sa morsure m'engourdit avec délice.

  VII

70 Qu'ils soient néant les distraits aux yeux blancs de perle
  Qu'ils soient néant les yeux et les oreilles, la tête qui ne prend racine
  dans la poitrine, et bien plus bas jusqu'à la racine du ventre.
  Car à quoi bon le manche sans la lame et la fleur sans le fruit?
  Mais vous ô jeunes feuilles, chantez la victoire du Lion dans l'humide
  soleil de Juin
  Je dis chantez le diamant qui naît des cendres de la Mort
75 O chantez la Présente qui nourrit le Poète du lait noir de l'amour.
  Vous êtes belles jeunes filles, et vos gorges d'or jeunes feuilles par la
  voix du Poète.
  Les mots s'envolent et se froissent au souffle du Vent d'Est, comme les
  monuments des hommes sous les bombes soufflantes
  Mais le poème est lourd de lait et le coeur du Poète brûle un feu sans
  poussière.

A New York

(pour un orchestre de jazz: solo de trompette)

I

New York! D'abord j'ai été confondu par ta beauté, ces grandes filles
   d'or aux jambes longues.
Si timide d'abord devant tes yeux de métal bleu, ton sourire de givre
Si timide. Et l'angoisse au fond des rues à gratte-ciel
Levant des yeux de chouette parmi l'éclipse du soleil.
5 Sulfureuse ta lumière et les fûts livides, dont les têtes foudroient le
   ciel
Les gratte-ciel qui défient les cyclones sur leurs muscles d'acier et leur
   peau patinée de pierres.
Mais quinze jours sur les trottoirs chauves de Manhattan
– C'est au bout de la troisième semaine que vous saisit la fièvre en un
   bond de jaguar
Quinze jours sans un puits ni pâturage, tous les oiseaux de l'air
10 Tombant soudain et morts sous les hautes cendres des terrasses.
Pas un rire d'enfant en fleur, sa main dans ma main fraîche
Pas un sein maternel, des jambes de nylon. Des jambes et des seins
   sans sueur ni odeur.
Pas un mot tendre en l'absence de lèvres, rien que des coeurs
   artificiels payés en monnaie forte
Et pas un livre où lire la sagesse. La palette du peintre fleurit des
   cristaux de corail.
15 Nuits d'insomnie ô nuits de Manhattan! si agitées de feux follets,
   tandis que les klaxons hurlent des heures vides
Et que les eaux obscures charrient des amours hygiéniques, tels des
   fleuves en crue des cadavres d'enfants.

II

Voici le temps des signes et des comptes
New York! Or voici le temps de la manne et de l'hysope.
Il n'est que d'écouter les trombones de Dieu, ton coeur battre au
   rythme du sang ton sang.
20 J'ai vu dans Harlem bourdonnant de bruits de couleurs solennelles et
   d'odeurs flamboyantes

– C'est l'heure du thé chez le livreur-en-produits-pharmaceutiques

J'ai vu se préparer la fête de la Nuit à la fuite du jour. Je proclame la Nuit plus véridique que le jour.

C'est l'heure pure où dans les rues, Dieu fait germer la vie d'avant mémoire

Tous les éléments amphibies rayonnants comme des soleils.

25 Harlem Harlem! voici ce que j'ai vu Harlem Harlem! Une brise verte de blés sourdre des pavés labourés par les pieds nus de danseurs Dans

Croupes ondes de soie et seins de fers de lance, ballets de nénuphars et de masques fabuleux

Aux pieds des chevaux de police, les mangues de l'amour rouler des maisons basses.

Et j'ai vu le long des trottoirs, des ruisseaux de rhum blanc des ruisseaux de lait noir dans le brouillard bleu des cigares.

J'ai vu le ciel neiger au soir des fleurs de coton et des ailes de séraphins et des panaches de sorciers.

30 Ecoute New York! ô écoute ta voix mâle de cuivre ta voix vibrante de hautbois, l'angoisse bouchée de tes larmes tomber en gros caillots de sang

Ecoute au loin battre ton coeur nocturne, rythme et sang du tam-tam, tam-tam sang et tam-tam.

III

New York! je dis New York, laisse affluer le sang noir dans ton sang

Qu'il dérouille tes articulations d'acier, comme une huile de vie

Qu'il donne à tes ponts la courbe des croupes et la souplesse des lianes.

35 Voici revenir les temps très anciens, l'unité retrouvée la réconciliation du Lion du Taureau et de l'Arbre

L'idée liée à l'acte l'oreille au coeur le signe au sens.

Voilà tes fleuves bruissants de caïmans musqués et de lamantins aux yeux de mirages. Et nul besoin d'inventer les Sirènes.

Mais il suffit d'ouvrir les yeux à l'arc-en-ciel d'Avril

Et les oreilles, surtout les oreilles à Dieu qui d'un rire de saxophone créa le ciel et la terre en six jours.

40 Et le septième jour, il dormit du grand sommeil nègre.

(*pour kôra*)

Comme rosée du soir, ton épître a fait mes yeux frais mon coeur.
Je l'ai lue à mes hôtes, à l'heure du thé sous la tente du Tagant.
Ils étaient de noble lignage, et maîtres de langage. J'en ai lu les
    feuillets qui pouvaient être lus
Réservant pour la veille ceux qui sont les plus délicats, comme la bosse
    du grand mâle
5 Et secrets. Et ce fut honneur à mon nom.

Mon désir est de mieux apprendre ton pays de t'apprendre.
Grâces pour ton épître son dire et sa substance
Et cet hiver que tu me rends présent, mais dont tu me défends
    comme une fourrure précieuse
M'en nommant le signe et le sens, la neige qui flamboie de mille feux
10 Brûlant le poids du corps, faisant l'esprit aigu le coeur candide.
Et mon pays de sel et ton pays de neige chantent à l'unisson.
Mais ta prudence est grande, mes forces faibles.
Il y a ta bonté marine comme un fjord de douceur, et le sapin qui
    reste vert sous la mort blanche
Debout dans la tempête. Il veille quand tremblent les bouleaux
15 Tandis que hurlent loups et lynx.
Grâces à la Princesse qui se faisait loisirs de mes récits, pleurant aux
    malheurs de ma race:
Les guerres contre l'Almamy, la ruine d'Elissa et l'exil à Djilôr du
    Saloum
La fondation du Sine. Et le désastre
Quand les Guelwârs furent couchés sous les canons comme des gerbes
    lourdes. Les cavaliers désarçonnés
20 Tombèrent debout les yeux grands ouverts au chant des griots.
Et de nouveau la ruine de Djilôr, le manoir investi par cactées et
    khakhams.
Dedans les punaises des bois font leur travail perfide, les reptiles
    paressent sur les lits de parade
Les portes battent longuement par les nuits de tornade.
Et cet autre exil plus dur à mon coeur, l'arrachement de soi à soi
25 A la langue de ma mère, au crâne de l'Ancêtre, au tam-tam de mon
    âme...
Je dis grâces à la Princesse qui annonça la résurrection de Djilôr.

J'arriverai à la fin de l'Eté.

Le ciel de ton esprit, le pays haut de ta prestance, la nuit bleue de ton
    coeur

Me seront fêtes à la fin de l'Initiation. Tu es mon univers.

30   Voici l'arc-en-ciel sur l'Hiver comme ton oriflamme.

Tu m'ouvres le visage de mes frères les hommes-blancs

Car ton visage est un chef-d'oeuvre, ton corps un paysage.

Tes yeux d'or vert qui changent comme la mer sous le soleil

Tes oreilles d'orfèvrerie, tes poignets de cristal

35   Ton nez d'aigle marin, tes reins de femme forte mon appui

Et ta démarche de navire oh! le vent dans les voiles de misaine…

Mais garde-moi Princesse de la tempête de tes narines

Qui barrissent comme des phoques; et je trébuche sur les rochers.

Je danserai devant toi la danse de la tornade.

40   L'impatience me presse de ses éperons d'acier.

Il me faut refroidir hâ! ce sang de poulain.

(*pour kôras et balafong*)

Princesse, ton épître m'est parvenue au coeur des pays hauts, entre
    Gambie et Casamance.

Je séjournais chez les hôtes héréditaires, la moitié de mon sang et la
    plus claire certes.

Et je m'enchantais comme toi 21 rue Poussin – mains subtiles épaule
    lilas!

Je m'enchantais aux jeux de cette langue labile avec des glissements
    sur l'aile

5   Langue qui chante sur trois tons, si tissée d'homéotéleutes et d'alliéra-
    tions, de douces implosives coupées de coups de glotte comme de
    navette

Musclée et maigre, je dis parcimonieuse, où les mots sans ciment sont
    liés par leur poids.

Dans le frais de la case, tu déviderais les énigmes parmi les princes de
    l'euphuïsme.

Princesse de Belborg, ton épître m'a frappé au coeur gauche.

Je l'ai bien entendue. C'était une nuit transparente, à l'heure où mon
    coeur veille sans parasites.

10   Voilà donc que les tigres vont sillonnant le ciel, plus lisses que
         l'anguille et plus plats qu'une lame.
     Ils se jouent du son et de la lumière, ils défient les sextants sur les
         observatoires.
     A distance, ils foudroient les escadres, sans éclair sans éclat.
     Les Prophètes debout sur les montagnes les avaient annoncés
     Les squales terribles du ciel sans ailes et sans coeur, mais bordés
         d'yeux ouverts.

15   'Ce fut l'an de la Découverte. De leurs yeux ils crachèrent un feu
         jaune. Et les eaux des fleuves roulèrent de l'or et des sueurs. Les
         Métropoles en furent gorgées. Les hommes nus furent réduits en
         esclavage, et les parents vendirent leurs enfants pour une pièce de
         Guinée.
     'Et ce fut l'an de la Raison. De leurs yeux ils crachèrent un feu rouge.
         Et la haine poussa au cou des hommes en ganglions noueux, et
         dans la boue du sang les soldats se baignèrent.
     On décora les bourreaux et savants; ils avaient inventé de tuer deux
         fois l'homme.
     'Ce sera l'an de la Technique. De leurs yeux ils cracheront un feu
         blanc. Les éléments se sépareront et s'agrégeront selon de mys-
         térieuses attirances et répulsions. Le sang des animaux et la sève des
         plantes seront de petit lait. Les blancs seront jaunes, les jaunes
         seront blancs, tous seront stériles.
     'Et l'on entendra dans les airs la voix unique du Dieu juste.'

20   Or le deuil du Septentrion sera mon deuil. J'ai offert mes yeux à la
         nuit pour que vive Paris.
     Je me rappelle rue Gît-le-Coeur, lorsque tu levais ton visage, ce front
         de pierre et de patine sous l'hiver blond
     Et cette voix grave de toutes les angoisses, mais comme le grondement
         des cascades généreuse à l'aube du monde
     Et tes yeux comme la lumière sur les collines bleues d'Assise
     Ta voix tes yeux qui chaque jour me faisaient naître.

25   J'ai grand besoin des murmures de Mai à Montsouris, de la splendeur
         des Tuileries à la fin de l'Eté
     Ou simplement, sous broussailles et lianes pour retrouver mon obélis-
         que, de l'angle pur du front de la Concorde.
     Princesse retiens ce message. Vends manoir terres et troupeaux. Vains
         seront les paratonnerres.

Abandonne ton père abandonne ta mère. Les morts iront avec les
morts. Et nous avons choisi de vivre.

Pas sur ces terres hautes hâ! surtout pas ici. S'en sont allés les temps
des charades et des lilas.

30   Nous brûlerons nos campements de la Belle Saison, nous descendrons
les fleuves

Au pays de ma mère, la mésopotamie où le sol est bien noir et le sang
sombre et l'huile épaisse.

Les hommes y sont de quatre coudées. Il ne distinguent pas leur
gauche de leur droite, ils ont neuf noms pour nommer le palmier
mais le palmier n'est pas nommé.

Je te recevrai sur la rive adverse, monté sur un quadrige de pirogues
et coiffé de la mitre double, ambassadeur de la Nuit et du Lion-
levant.

Je le sais bien ce pays n'est pas noble, qui est du jour troisième, eau et
terre à moitié.

35   Ma noblesse est de vivre cette terre, Princesse selon cette terre

Comme le riz l'igname la palme et le palétuvier, l'ancêtre Lamantin
l'ancêtre Crocodile

Et Lilanga ma soeur. Elle danse elle vit.

Car comment vivre sinon dans l'Autre au fil de l'Autre, comme l'arbre
déraciné par la tornade et les rêves des îles flottantes?

Et pourquoi vivre si l'on ne danse l'Autre?

40   Lilanga, ses pieds sont deux reptiles, des mains qui massent des pilons
qui battent des mâles qui labourent.

Et de la terre sourd le rythme, sève et sueur, une onde odeur de sol
mouillé

Qui trémule les jambes de statue, les cuisses ouvertes au secret

Déferle sur la croupe, creuse les reins tend ventre gorges et collines

Proues de tam-tams. Les tam-tams se réveillent, Princesse, les tam-
tams nous réveillent. Les tam-tams nous ouvrent l'aorte.

45   Les tam-tams roulent, les tam-tams roulent, au gré du coeur. Mais les
tam-tams galopent hô! les tam-tams galopent.

Princesse, nos épaules roulent sous les vagues, nos épaules de feuilles
tremblent sous le cyclone

Nos lianes nagent dans l'onde, nos mains s'ouvrent nénuphars, et
chantent les alizés dans nos doigts de filaos.

Mais lumière sur nos visages plus beaux que masques d'or!...

Princesse, nous serons maîtres de la Mort.

50 Retiens ce message Princesse, nous serons le Ciel et la Terre.
(*pour khalam*)

Je ne sais en quels temps c'était, je confonds toujours l'enfance et
l'Eden
Comme je mêle la Mort et la Vie – un pont de douceur les relie.

Or je revenais de Fa'oye, m'étant abreuvé à la tombe solennelle
Comme les lamantins s'abreuvent à la fontaine de Simal.
5 Or je revenais de Fa'oye, et l'horreur était au zénith
Et c'était l'heure où l'on voit les Esprits, quand la lumière est trans-
parente
Et il fallait s'écarter des sentiers, pour éviter leur main fraternelle et
mortelle.
L'âme d'un village battait à l'horizon. Etait-ce des vivants ou des
Morts?

'Puisse mon poème de paix être l'eau calme sur tes pieds et ton visage
10 'Et que l'ombre de notre cour soit fraîche à ton coeur', me dit-elle.
Ses mains polies me revêtirent d'un pagne de soie et d'estime
Son discours me charma de tout mets délectable – douceur du lait de
la mi-nuit
Et son sourire était plus mélodieux que le khalam de son dyâli.
L'étoile du matin vint s'asseoir parmi nous, et nous pleurâmes
délicieusement.

15 – Ma soeur exquise, garde donc ces grains d'or, qu'ils chantent l'éclat
sombre de ta gorge.
Ils étaient pour ma fiancée belle, et je n'avais pas de fiancée.
– Mon frère élu, dis-moi ton nom. Il doit résonner haut comme un
sorong
Rutiler comme le sabre au soleil. Oh! chante seulement ton nom.
Mon coeur est un coffret de bois précieux, ma tête un vieux parchemin de Djenné.
20 Chante seulement ton lignage, que ma mémoire te réponde.

Je ne sais en quels temps c'était, je confonds toujours présent et passé
Comme je mêle la Mort et la Vie – un pont de douceur les relie.

(*pour orgues, et tam-tam au loin*)

Laetare Jerusalem et... Je dis bien *laetare* mon coeur
Vide et vaste comme une pièce froide – mais larmes Seigneur dans
  tes mains si calmes.
Laetare sur l'aile neigeuse des toits hauts quand fulmine son visage
  d'aurore.

Laetare sur l'Eglise au lait doux de coco et sur son visage pascal.
5 Blancs sont les enfants blancs les hommes, et les femmes de grandes
   fleurs
Fragrantes de pagnes et de boubous, et mon amour l'étoile sur la nuit
  des gorges.
Par les voix de jour par les voix de joie, *laetare* par myrrhe et encens
Par le fumet des viandes riches et par la transe des danses sérères.

Seigneur *laetare* dans mon coeur, comme un dimanche d'Europe au
  réveil.
10 Je suis plein de ténèbres mon Dieu. Brise la boîte maléfique
Et brise mon coeur, qu'il s'effeuille en purs pétales de chant.

(*pour flûtes*)

Une main de lumière a caressé mes paupières de nuit
Et ton sourire s'est levé sur les brouillards qui flottaient monotones
  sur mon Congo.
Mon coeur a fait écho au chant virginal des oiseaux d'aurore
Tel mon sang qui rythmait jadis le chant blanc de la sève dans les
  branches de mes bras.
5 Voici la fleur de brousse et l'étoile dans mes cheveux et le bandeau
   qui ceint le front du pâtre-athlète.
J'emprunterai la flûte qui rythme la paix des troupeaux
Et tout le jour assis à l'ombre de tes cils, près de la Fontaine Fimla
Fidèle, je paîtrai les mugissements blonds de tes troupeaux.
Car ce matin une main de lumière a caressé mes paupières de nuit
10 Et tout le long du jour, mon coeur a fait écho au chant virginal des
   oiseaux.

(*pour khalam*)

Ton visage beauté des temps anciens! Sortons les pagnes par-
fumés aux tons passés.
Mémoire des temps sans histoire! C'était avant notre naisance.

Nous revenions de Dyônewâr, nos pensées s'attardaient sur les
bolongs
Où luisaient, faible écho de soie, les ailes des éloges cadencés.
5 Les bêtes des palétuviers les guettaient dans l'extase à leur
passage
Et les étoiles sur la mer concave étaient un autre écho divin
Et les rames mélodieuses et lentes ruisselaient d'étoiles filantes.
Comme une statue, un masque de proue penché sur l'abîme
sonore
Tu chantais d'une voix d'ombre *ndeïsane!* la gloire du Champion debout.
10 Les bêtes des palétuviers buvaient délices! ton souffle liquide.
Nous revenions de Dyônewâr par les bolongs et vaguement.
Lors ton visage d'aujourd'hui sous sa patine avait la beauté
noire de l'Eternel.

(*pour tama*)

Ton nom ne m'est pas inconnu, aigrette de Satang et de Sitôr.
Il est venu de loin, tout chargé des parfums de Pount
Porté par la bouche des piroguiers et des chameliers au long curs.

Tu n'es pas le village ouvert que l'on met à genoux avec quelques
pétards
5 Tandis que se lamentent longuement les mères, comme les chacals sur
les tanns.
Tu n'es pas la vierge que l'on attrait avec une maigre louange
Et trois violoneux en chômage, enfilant des perles de traite.

Tu es le tata qui voit de loin venir la poussière de sang des chevaux-
du-Fleuve

Tu es le tata qui domine les ruses bleues des cavaliers masqués.

10 Et il me faut tout l'art des Peuples-de-la-Mer, il me faut la puissance des canons.

Tu es le Serpent Sacré qui ne parle, ô belle poseuse d'énigmes

Mais des Maîtres-de-science, j'ai appris à percer les hiéroglyphes sur le sable.

Toi Ange de l'Enfant Prodigue, Ange des solutions à la clarté de l'aube

Quand les brouillards toute la nuit hâ! ont pesé profonds sur mon angoisse.

15 Tu es la porte de beauté, la porte radieuse de grâce

A l'entrée du temps primordial. Et je jouais avec les cailloux et colombes.

Signare, je chanterai ta grâce ta beauté.

Des maîtres de Dyong j'ai appris l'art de tisser des paroles plaisantes

Paroles de pourpre à te parer, Princesse noire d'Elissa.

(*pour deux flûtes*)

Lasse ma tête mienne-ci, lourdes mes pensées à la chaîne

Mes nerfs las dans l'usine tournant au café – Seigneur ce tremblement qui taraude mes os!

Lasses lasses mes jambes lasses par les rues de thé à cinq heures.

Et mon coeur de ma mère lasse, qui oscille toujours entre Espoir et Angoisse.

5 Je rêve le soir d'amuissement à la finale des Nations.

Ma tête sur le sable de ton sein mes yeux dans tes yeux d'Outre-mer

Quand les piroguiers de la Grand-Mer nous livreront-ils les poissons du rêve?

Notre pagne est d'or blanc, d'or rouge les nuages notre haut pavillon seigneurial.

Vois les deux cités soeurs par delà le bolong, la pourpre des vivants la cité bleue des Morts.

10 Je rêve le soir d'un pays perdu, où les Rois et les Morts étaient mes familiers.

Soufflent tes mains leurs alizés dans mes cheveux, qui bruissent de
   délices.
Oh! leur chant dans les hautes palmes ou sur l'aile des göelands, je ne
   sais trop.
Que je dorme sur la paix de ton sein, dans l'odeur des pommes-
   canelles.
Nous boirons le lait de la lune, qui ruisselle sur la sable de minuit.

(pour deux flûtes et un tamtam lointain)   *A James Benoit*

Etait-ce une nuit maghrebine? – Je laisse Mogador aux filles de
   platine.
Etait-ce une nuit maghrebine? C'était aussi la Nuit notre nuit
   joalienne
D'avant notre naissance l'ineffable nuit: tu te coiffais devant le
   miroir de mes yeux.

Nous étions assis dans l'angoisse, à l'ombre de notre secret
5 Dans cette angoisse de l'attente qui faisait frémir tes narines.
Te la rappelles-tu cette rumeur de paix? De la ville basse vague
   par vague
Elle venait battre à nos pieds. Un phare au loin appelait à ma
   droite
A gauche tout près de mon coeur, l'étrange immobilité de tes
   yeux.
Ah! ces éclairs soudain dans la nuit d'hivernage – je pouvais lire
   ton visage
10 Et je buvais ton visage terrible à longs traits altérés qui incen-
   diaient ma soif
Et dans mon coeur qui s'étonnait, dans mon coeur de silence
   qui n'en pouvait mais
Cette rafale d'aboiements là-bas, qui l'éclataient comme
   grenade.

Puis ce crissement mordoré du sable, ce battement palpébral
   dans les feuilles.
   4   IPS

Des gardes noirs passaient dieux géants de l'Eden: des noctuelles visage de lune
15 Pesaient doucement à leur bras – leur bonheur nous était
brûlure.
En écoutant nos coeurs, on les entendait battre là-bas du côté
de Fadioutt
On entendait frémir la terre sous les pieds vainqueurs des
athlètes
La voix de l'Amante chanter la splendeur ténébreuse de
l'Amant.
Et nous n'osions bouger nos mains tremblantes, et nos lèvres
s'ouvraient et se fermaient.
20 Si l'aigle se jetait soudain sur nos poitrines, avec un cri sauvage
de comète!...
Mais m'emportait irrésistible le courant, vers l'horrible chant
des écueils de tes yeux.

Nous aurons d'autres nuits Sopé: tu reviendras sur ce banc
d'ombre
Tu seras la même toujours et tu ne seras pas la même.
Qu'importe? A travers tes métamorphoses, j'adorerai le visage
de Koumba Tâm.

Elégie de minuit

Eté splendide Eté, qui nourris le Poète du lait de ta lumière
Moi qui poussais comme blé de Printemps, qui m'enivrais de la
verdeur de l'eau, du ruissellement vert dans l'or du Temps
Ah! plus ne peux supporter ta lumière, la lumière des lampes, ta
lumière atomique qui désintègre tout mon être
Plus ne peux supporter la lumière de minuit. La splendeur des
honneurs est comme un Sahara
5 Un vide immense, sans erg ni hamada sans herbe, sans un battement
de cils, sans un battement de coeur.
Donc vingt-quatre heures sur vingt-quatre, et les yeux grands ouverts
comme le Père Cloarec
Crucifié sur la pierre par les Païens de Joal adorateurs des Serpents.

Dans mes yeux le phare portugais qui tourne, oui vingt-quatre heures
  sur vingt-quatre
Une mécanique précise et sans répit, jusqu'à la fin des temps.

10 Je bondis de mon lit, un léopard sur le garrot, coup de Simoun
  soudain qui ensable ma gorge.
  – Ah! si seulement m'écrouler dans la fiente et le sang, dans le néant.
  Je tourne en rond parmi mes livres, qui me regardent du fond de
  leurs yeux
  Six mille lampes qui brûlent vingt-quatre heures sur vingt-quatre.
  Je suis debout, lucide étrangement lucide
15 Et je suis beau, comme le coureur de cent mètres, comme l'étalon noir
  en rut de Mauritanie.
  Je charrie dans mon sang un fleuve de semences à féconder toutes les
  plaines de Byzance
  Et les collines, les collines austères.
  Je suis l'Amant et la locomotive au piston bien huilé.

Douceur de ses lèvres de fraises, densité de son corps de pierre,
  douceur de son secret de pêche
20 Son corps, terre profonde ouverte au noir Semeur.
  L'Esprit germe sous l'aine, dans la matrice du désir
  Le sexe est une antenne au centre du Multiple, où s'échangent des
  messages fulgurants.
  Plus ne peut m'apaiser la musique d'amour, le rythme sacré du
  poème.
  Contre le désespoir Seigneur, j'ai besoin de toutes mes forces
25 – Douceur du poignard en plein coeur, jusqu'à la garde
  Comme un remords. Je ne suis pas sûr de mourir.
  Et si c'était cela l'Enfer, l'absence de sommeil ce désert du Poète
  Cette douleur de vivre, ce mourir de ne pas mourir
  L'angoisse des ténèbres, cette passion de mort et de lumière
30 Comme les phalènes la nuit sur les lampes-tempêtes, dans l'horrible
  pourrissement des forêts vierges.

Seigneur de la lumière et des ténèbres
Toi seigneur du Cosmos, fais que je repose sous Joal-l'Ombreuse
Que je renaisse au Royaume d'enfance bruissant de rêves

Que je sois le berger de ma bergère par les tanns de Dyilôr où
    fleurissent les Morts
35 Que j'éclate en applaudissements quand entrent dans le cercle
    Téning-N'dyaré et Tyagoum-N'dyaré
Que je danse comme l'Athléte au tamtam des Morts de l'année.
Ce n'est qu'une prière. Vous savez ma patience paysanne.
Viendra la paix viendra l'Ange de l'aube, viendra le chant des oiseaux
    inouïs
Viendra la lumière de l'aube.
40 Je dormirai du sommeil de la Mort qui nourrit le Poète
   – O Toi qui donne la maladie du sommeil aux nouvea-unés,
     à Marône la Poétesse à Kotye-Barma le Juste! –
Je dormirai à l'aube, ma poupée rose dans les bras
Ma poupée aux yeux vert et or, à la langue si merveilleuse
La langue même du poème.

Elégie des circoncis

Nuit d'enfance, Nuit bleue Nuit blonde ô Lune!
Combien de fois t'ai-je invoquée ô Nuit! pleurant au bord des routes
Au bord des douleurs de mon âge d'homme? Solitude! et c'est les
    dunes alentour.
Or c'était nuit d'enfance extrême, dense comme la poix. La peur
    courbait les dos sous les rugissements des lions
5 Courbait les hautes herbes le silence sournois de cette nuit.
Feu de branches toi feu d'espoir! pâle mémoire du Soleil qui rassurait
    mon innocence
A peine – il me fallait mourir. Je portais la main à mon cou, comme la
    vierge qui frissonne à l'horreur de la Mort.
Il me fallait Mourir à la beauté du chant – toutes choses dérivent au fil
    de la Mort.
Voyez le crépuscule à la gorge de tourterelle, quand roucoulent
    bleues les palombes
10 Et volent les mouettes du rêve avec des cris plaintifs.

Mourons et dansons coude à coude en une guirlande tressée

Que la robe n'emprisonne nos pas, mais rutile le don de la promise,
  éclairs sous les nuages.
Le tamtam laboure *woï!* le silence sacré. Dansons, le chant fouette le
  sang
Le rythme chasse cette angoisse qui nous tient à la gorge. La Vie tient
  la mort à distance.
15 Dansons au refrain de l'angoisse, que se lève la nuit du sexe dessus
  notre ignorance dessus notre innocence.
Ah! mourir à l'enfance, que meure le poème se désintègre la syntaxe,
  que s'abîment tous les mots qui ne sont pas essentiels.
Le poids du rythme suffit, pas besoin de mots-ciment pour bâtir sur le
  roc la Cité de demain.
Surgisse le Soleil de la mer des ténèbres
Sang! Les flots sont couleur d'aurore.

20 Mais Dieu, tant de fois ai-je lamenté – combien de fois? – les nuits
  d'enfance transparentes.
Midi-le-Mâle est l'heure des Esprits, où toute forme se dépouille de sa
  chair
Comme les arbes en Europe sous le soleil d'hiver.
Voilà, les os sont abstraits, ils ne se prêtent qu'aux calculs de la règle
  du compas du sextant.
La vie comme le sable s'échappe aux doigts de l'homme, les cristaux
  de neige emprisonnent la vie de l'eau
25 Le serpent de l'eau glisse aux mains vaines des roseaux.
Nuits chères Nuits amies, et Nuits d'enfance, parmi les tanns parmi
  les bois
Nuits palpitantes de présences, et de paupières, si peuplées d'ailes et
  de souffles
De silence vivant, dites combien de fois vous ai-je lamentées au mitan
  de mon âge?

Le poème se fane au soleil de Midi, il se nourrit de la rosée du soir
30 Et rythme le tamtam le battement de la sève sous le parfum des fruits
  mûrs.
Maître des Initiés, j'ai besoin je le sais de ton savoir pour percer le
  chiffre des choses
Prendre connaissance de mes fonctions de père et de lamarque

Mesurer exactement le champ de mes charges, répartir la moisson sans oublier un ouvrier ni orphelin.

Le chant n'est pas que charme, il nourrit les têtes laineuses de mon troupeau.

35 Le poème est oiseau-serpent, les noces de l'ombre et de la lumière à l'aube

Il monte Phénix! il chante les ailes déployées, sur le carnage des paroles.

NOTES TO THE POEMS

Lettre à un poète

This poem breaks into three recognisable parts. The first eight lines are a eulogy of the poet Aimé Césaire; the next sixteen, carrying further the eulogy, elaborate Senghor's ideas of the proper subject matter and method of the black poet; the last section gives the poem, conceived in terms of the traditional African feeling for nobility, a richly evocative conclusion. The poem, addressed to a colleague and close associate, is a statement by Senghor of his own ideas concerning his mission and his inspiration as a poet.

Note that the poem is rhymed in couplets throughout.

Dedication: Aimé Césaire: French Caribbean poet, b. 1913 in Martinique; reputed for the passionate quality of his work. See Introduction, p. 6 and p. 9.

2 *Les goélands noirs:* the black-backed gull is called the 'goéland à manteau noir'. The oblique reference to this bird captures in a vivid compact image the row of black oarsmen as they move swiftly and rhythmically down-river.

3 The line associates ideas and impressions of the different senses (synaesthesia; cf Baudelaire's warm spice-islands).

Rivières du Sud: French colonial term for all the rivers from the Saloum in Senegal to the Gabon in Equatorial Africa. Senghor designates the African part of the black world, in contrast to the Caribbean (the *Iles*)

5 *ruche de silence:* Césaire's disciples, clustered round him like a swarm of bees around their Queen, but in attentive silence; Césaire's poetry is thus a spiritual honey, distilled from a refined art, cf *la fleur de tes lèvres subtiles*, in l. 4.

6 The disciples do not drink till moonrise, like Muslims during the annual fast; the line suggests Césaire's spiritual leadership.

8 *sapotille:* the sapodilla plum (or naseberry) the fruit of an evergreen that grows in the tropical parts of America. It has a smooth velvety skin. (See also 'Femme noire', l. 7, for a similar image.)

9–10 The word order is inverted; in ordinary prose it would go 'La braise ardente, ta musique, me charme...' Césaire's poetic ardour (*la braise ardente*) has cooled (hence *cendre*); Senghor can only recapture its original warmth by an effort of memory (recalling its earlier effect), like a man drawing closer to a dying fire. By implication

Césaire is asked to write poetry of the kind he used to write. (Césaire had not in fact lost his poetic powers.)

11-12   the themes and proccupations of the black poet, opposed to the conventions of Western lyricism. For the same contrast, see 'Que m'accompagnent kôras et balafong' (stanzas III and IV).

13   *fruits blancs de ton jardin:* only the distinctive fruits of the poetic mind are fit offerings to the gods.

14   *la fleur...du mil fin:* the poet is nourished on the best of the land. Millet is a staple diet in Senegal and the West African savannah.

18   Césaire as a spiritual hero with supernatural attributes, associated with night, the symbol of the spiritual reality of the universe. For the symbolic quality of night in Senghor, see 'Nuit de Sine', ll. 11-12, and also stanza IX of 'Kôras et balafong'.

20   *ton vers est la respiration de la nuit:* African in origin, Césaire captures in poetry the rhythms and mystic life of the African night with which Senghor identifies the West Indies.

21   *princes légitimes:* as opposed to the French colonial rulers.

23   *Rythmique à contre-temps:* the 'off-beat' (syncopation) that characterises jazz, to whose rhythmic structure Senghor likens traditional African oral poetry. The enjambement produces the same effect.
     les pauvres...gain d'une année: Senegalese peasants customarily offer annual tributes out of their harvest to the local aristocracy.

24   *leur coeur d'ambre:* amber is a translucent warm yellow-brown. The image suggests glowing simplicity of the heart as a jewel-like tribute.

26   *côtre:* sailing vessel.
     kaïcédrat: a Senegalese tree, of royal significance.

27-8   Césaire should return to the sources of his poetic inspiration and racial identity, like a prince to his domain: he will be assured of a royal welcome.

27   *festin des prémisses:* festivals held in African societies at the sowing or harvesting of crops; Césaire will regain his poetic power and return to his vocation as black poet.
     soleil déclive: setting sun.

28   *athlètes:* here, wrestlers, the traditional sporting heroes of Senegal.

Nuit de Sine

This poem combines pure evocation with symbolic expression. Both aspects are developed through the image of night, the fundamental reference for Senghor's poetic vision (see Introduction, p. 27). The related theme of devotion to the ancestors is extended to express cosmic renewal.

The four stanzas of the poem move through a succession of evocations to the final statement. The first stanza sets the scene of restful meditation at the end of the day. The second introduces concrete details into its village setting, leading into the broader third stanza, with its deliberate *rapprochement* of the elemental and the human, to reflect the all-pervasive influence of night. The last stanza draws out the immediate personal significance of the symbol for the poet in relation to his ancestors, and its ultimate meaning in his vision of the universe.

Title: Sine: a river in Senegal. The Serer, Senghor's ethnic group, inhabit the basin formed by the confluence of the two rivers, Sine and Saloum (see map).

  1 *Femme, pose sur mon front:* woman addressed as the principle of life (see 'Femme
      noire')
      mains balsamiques: with the soothing power of balsam.
2–4 Note the sibilants (the breeze), and the quiet measured pace, with its pauses and
      renewals.
  4 *le silence rythmé:* muted beat of far-off drums punctuating the silence of the African
      night, as well as the breath of mystic presences.
5–6 the atmosphere of the vast mystery of night. The pace quickens and broadens; the
      nasals weave a pattern of assonances which combine with the plosives to suggest
      depth and resonance.
  5 *sang sombre:* cf Introduction, pp. 24–25.
  6 *brume des villages perdus:* suggests the remoteness of Africa to him, obscured by the
      mists of his exile.
7–10 Note the effect of the sound values in the creation of atmosphere; the stanza is
      structured in parallelisms.
  8 *les conteurs:* of folk tales (*contes*), usually told after dark, with song and dance (l. 10).
 10 The line has two equal parts of eleven syllables, with a break (caesura) after the first
      verb; the movement suggests the 'dragging' effect.
11–14 The interplay of light and darkness produces an effect of suffused luminosity. The
      contrasted but complementary aspects of the physical world point to the unity of the
      universe; this is given more fundamental expression in l. 21.
 11 *la Nuit qui songe:* cf Baudelaire, 'la douce Nuit qui marche' in his 'Recueillement'. The
      image is built on an inversion of ideas which reinforces the personification of night.
      Night is shown serenely reclining in 'Kôras et balafong' (l. 44).
 12 *long pagne de lait:* the Milky way, with which the moon appears to be robed.
      (*Pagne* = French–African word for printed cloth.)
 13 the para-rime *toits/étoiles* suggests the dialogue.
 14 *le foyer:* hearth, fire lit to warm the household, especially during the Harmattan, the
      cold Saharan wind.
      âcres et douces: harmony of contrasts.
 15 *la lampe au beurre clair:* the lamp-oil is shea butter; a homely image which carries the
      idea of spiritual illumination.
      les ancêtres, le parents, les enfants: 'the dead, the living and the unborn' – the unbroken
      progression of life traditional in the thought of African societies.
 16 *Elissa:* village in Guinea Bissau, south of Senegal, where Senghor's ancestors are
      buried.
 17 *Ils n'ont pas voulu…torrent séminal:* traditional societies see the bearing of offspring as
      a way of perpetuating oneself. After *Comme nous exilés*, l. 16, this suggests the poet's
      anguish at the diminution of his authentic self, his aspiration to a plentitude of being,
      forcefully affirmed in l. 21.
 18 *âmes propices:* the dead, watching over the destinies of their living descendants.
 19 *dang:* a cereal meal.
 20 Note the obsessive pattern of the subjunctives.
 21 The run-on from the previous line emphasises the verb *Vivre.*
      avant de descendre…: refers back to the sinking moon in l. 7 (here *le plongeur*), and
      gathers up the thought into a final statement. The poet aspires to intensity of life
      before his plunge into the ultimate sleep of death, which will take him to his

ancestors and is thus a new state of life beyond the physical, a conversion of his being into the eternity of the race. In *les hautes profondeurs du sommeil* this personal reference acquires a wider meaning. The continuity between the height of the heavens and the depth of the sea indicates the unity of the universe, whose physical and spiritual reality are based on a cyclic principle (night follows day, which gives way to night; the sinking moon disappears to return later); so all life is a constant renewal, and flows from an essential permanence of being.

Joal

Joal, Senghor's birthplace, is a coastal village just south of Dakar (see map). In this poem on the nostalgic recollection of childhood, Joal symbolises the poet's *royaume d'enfance*.

Form and diction are simple, as befits the theme, carried by the refrain *Je me rappelle:* the poet casts his mind back to the wonder of his childhood which he contrasts to the present misery of his exile. See also Camara Laye's *L'Enfant Noir* (ed. Joyce Hutchinson, Cambridge 1966).

3   *les signares:* from the Portuguese word *senhora* (French *madame*); ladies of the local bourgeoisie, in particular the mulatto ladies of Saint Louis, former capital of Senegal. *l'ombre verte des vérandas:* the colour of the foliage transferred to the shade it provides. Perhaps an unconscious memory of Verlaine; cf *l'ombre verte des arbres* in 'Nuit du Walpurgis classique'.

4   *Yeux surréels:* cf Introduction, p. 23.

6   Koumba N'Dofène, the last king of Sine. After his death in 1925, the protectorate of Sine was merged with the colony of Senegal by the French. He was a relative of Senghor's father, whom he sometimes visited. His imposing figure and the pomp of these ceremonial visits left a deep impression on Senghor (see also 'Kôras et balafong', stanza v).

7–10   The Serers have been converted to Christianity in significant numbers. These lines suggest that the conversion leaves the African animist beliefs largely unaffected.

7   Note the expressive sonorities; the reference is to a pagan sacrifice.

8   *griot:* poet, storyteller, praise-singer, entertainer, the *griot* (or *dyali*) still remains in most parts of the Sudanese region of West Africa the principal curator and repository of oral tradition.

9   *les voix païennes:* African Christians give a strongly accented rhythm to Gregorian chant, normally sung in an even, solemn manner. The *Tantum Ergo* is the Latin hymn sung at the evening office (Benediction), when the Host is exposed.

10   On Palm Sunday fresh palm fronds are carried in religious processions.

12   *Les choeurs de lutte:* teams of wrestlers, the national sport in Senegal; matches are accompanied by elaborate social ceremonies.

13   Note the enjambement.
Kor Siga: an exclamation of admiration addressed to wrestlers. *Kor* means 'man', and the term implies valiant qualities. *Siga* is the name of a woman with whom the champion is associated; the whole expression signifies 'protector of Siga'. Among the Serer, praises are chanted to wrestlers; they are referred to as the champions of their sisters or of their beloved one, the idea being that they are defending their honour before the women. Cf *Kor Sanou*, in 'A l'appel de la race de Saba', stanza vi.

17 *jazz orphelin:* an allusion to the Negro spiritual 'Sometimes I feel like a motherless child' also expressing solitude in exile. The line establishes a parallel between the condition of the black man in America, and that of the colonised assimilated African.

Femme noire

This poem derives in part from the Western convention of the love poem; it is a hymn of praise to a loved woman. Senghor gives the subject an original dimension. The woman addressed is not an individual but a symbolic African woman, incarnating the enduring qualities of the race. She is woman as lover, who calls forth erotic feelings, as mother, who evokes filial sentiments, and as Africa itself, source of the race and its organic bond with the life of the universe. The three meanings are closely interwoven; the thematic development evokes multiple responses which deepen its effect and significance.

The poem combines the enumerative style of the Western canticle (as in the Catholic litany), and the African praise poem. It remains essentially a lyrical work, in which the refrains introduce impressionistic invocations in which Senghor develops a succession of ecstatic images. The final stanza is an exultant affirmation of the power of the poet's art and of its vital significance.

1 *Femme nue:* natural, unadorned; cf *corps dépouillé*, 'Kôras et balafong', l. 38.
2 *ta couleur qui est vie:* the immediate reference is to the colour of the African woman which has the value of fecundity and symbolises fullness of life. But the landscape image introduced at l. 4 with *Terre promise* suggests that he may also mean the green of vegetation, expressive of the luxuriant natural life of Africa.
    ta forme qui est beauté: a reference to sculpture as visual form and spiritual reference. The idea here underlies ll. 9 and 17, and is developed in 'Kôras et balafong', ll. 145–8.
3 The poet's mother as representative African woman, and as a figure of the African continent; cf 'A l'appel de la race de Saba'.
4 *au coeur de l'Eté et de Midi:* at the sun's zenith, the period of maturity. *Eté* is the high point of the year as *Midi* is of the day (cf Claudel's *Partage de Midi*). The brilliant imagery contrasts with the sombreness of the previous line, and prepares the revelation in the next.
5 *l'éclair d'un aigle:* the compelling force of the poet's illumination.
6 *femme obscure:* dark, mysterious, bearer of the secrets of life.
7 *Fruit mûr à la chair ferme:* maturity of body and spirit.
    vin noir: the very essence of the race. Cf *sang sombre, lait noir*, etc. (see Introduction, p. 25).
8 *savane qui frémis... Vent d'Est:* the intensity of the cosmic life expressed in erotic terms; the seasonal Harmattan blows into Senegal from the east.
10 *Ta voix grave de contre-alto...:* possibly an allusion to the American Negro singer, Marian Anderson, famous for singing Negro spirituals (cf *chant spirituel*).
12 *Huile que ne ride nul souffle:* smoothness of skin expressive of spiritual composure. Oil also suggests sacredness; oil is used to anoint.
    Mali: the old Mali empire.
    The line divides into three equal parts of eight syllables giving expressive regularity of movement.

13 *Gazelle aux attaches célestes:* the gazelle is swift and elegant – the black woman as a legendary creature with supernatural powers.

14–15 The visual imagery is based on the contrasting play of light and darkness conveying the poet's mental states.

14 *qui se moire:* with a shimmering lustre, like watered silk.

17–18 The poem converges upon these two lines. The first, with its echo of l. 2, takes up the sculptural theme and gives it the wider connotation of art as expression of eternal truths. The final line develops the notion of woman as the channel of the continuity of the race, intimately related to the Earth. The line emphasises the idea of life as a continuous process, the theme of renewal and rebirth.

Neige sur Paris

A poem dominated by bitterness. It contrasts the ideals of Western civilisation – especially peace and universal brotherhood, the message of Christmas – and the reality of Europe in the winter of 1938; the tensions that were to lead to the Second World War.

In the second stanza Senghor passes from the internal disorders of Europe to its ravages abroad, and its assault upon Africa. The two aspects are related; the stanza is thus an indictment. Although the poet moves to a statement of Christian forgiveness, and a reaffirmation of universal love, the poem demonstrates Senghor's ambivalence towards a society in which he is involved but remains an outsider.

There is a corresponding ambivalence in the imagery, with its variations on the motif of whiteness (the leading image is of snow), and the contrasts and oppositions through which the poet leads his imagery, to be resolved in the religious sentiment underlying the whole, and the personal attachment stated at the end. 'Neige sur Paris' looks forward to the volume *Hosties Noires*, in particular its concluding poem, 'Prière de paix'.

1–4 The winter snow is used both as a figure of the Western world's numbing effect upon the poet's soul, and as a symbol of mortification and purification.

4 *la mort blanche:* not just absence of life: an image of the ominous presage of war.

5–6 an ironic reference to European materialism; even the factories seem to put out white flags of peace. See also l. 21 below.

9 *l'Espagne déchirée:* the Spanish civil war of 1936–39, generally seen as a forerunner of the Second World War.

10 *le Rebelle juif et catholique:* General Francisco Franco, who commanded the Falangist forces against the Republicans during the Spanish civil war, and established a dictatorship over the country until his death in 1975.

12 anticipates l. 24 in its readiness to forgive, though it leads directly to the catalogue of African grievances against Europe; hence the emotional tension within the poet.

14–21 the sufferings of the black race as a parallel to the passion of Christ, which is enacted anew. Note the repetition of *mains blanches*.

18 *rôniers:* species of tropical tree.

19 *les Saras:* an ethnic group in Chad distinguished for their tall straight physique; the men are identified with the trees of the preceding line.
vos mains brunes: God in his incarnation in Christ, who was a Jew and therefore dark in colour. See also 'A New York' which ends with a similar picture of God as non-white.

21 the ironical note of ll. 5–6 acquires a sharp edge.

23 *qui demain troqueront la chair noire:* colonialism assimilated to the degradation of black men during the slave trade.

24–6 The poet's heart is warmed by his individual understanding of Christ's message; the terms in which the reconciliation is stated convey nonetheless the sense of emotional effort.

27 *main de rosée:* a discreet reference to a white female companion whose affection offsets the poet's feeling of bitterness against her race in general: *main de rosée* (with its suggestion of *mains de rose*) attenuates the harsh association of *mains blanches*.

Prière aux masques

An invocation to the ancestral gods, calling their attention to the plight of Africa and asking for the moral strength needed by their children to carry out their mission to the world. The opening apostrophe expresses the significance of the masks as representations of the immaterial world beyond the visible; there follows the prayer itself; the last three lines affirm the spiritual energy of Africans.

In its vocabulary and solemn rhythm, the poem is religious, but in the animist tradition.

3 *aux quatre points:* the cardinal points.

5 *Ancêtre à tête de lion:* the mask represents, as image, the dead members of the family, whose spirits are sometimes identified with an animal-totem, considered in many traditional societies as the first ancestor and as the embodiment and protector of the race. (See also 'Le totem'). Senghor's father bore the Serer name *Diogoye* (lion) so he refers here to the ancestral symbol of his own family. Among the Serer and other peoples of Senegal, the lion represents nobility and courage.

6 *forclos:* an archaic equivalent for *interdit*, now only a legal term; here giving an emphatic and solemn tone. In most African societies, sacred places are forbidden to women and to uninitiated males.

tout sourire qui se fane: all that is frivolous and unenduring; contrast the previous line.

7 the function of the masks is to maintain spiritual communion between living and dead, and so the sacred continuity of society as a whole.

8 the masks are ageless; compare *vox yeux immuables* in l. 13.

9 The religious imagery shifts here, to an ironical assessment of Western knowledge expressing the poet's sense of his ambiguous situation. Book-knowledge, worshipped by the white man, is superficial; cf the opening lines of 'Congo'.

11 *l'agonie d'une princesse pitoyable:* the nobility of Africa in her present distress; the expression carries forward the idea of empires. For a more elaborate presentation, see 'Kôras et balafong', stanza VII.

12 perhaps Senghor's most vivid statement of the complementarity of the two worlds of Europe and Africa, and of his concern to see them bound in a living unity. Note the organic terms.

16 *le levain:* a biblical image. As leaven (yeast) makes sour white dough into good bread, so the spiritual influence of Africa will give new life to Europe and the world.

17–19 the spiritual mission of Africa, which Senghor seems to offer here less as an exaltation of Africa than as pitiful appraisal of the results of European civilisation.

20–2 the Europeans' negative view of Africa (a matter of economic exploitation) turned into positive affirmation. The association of Africans with death in the European imagination (through the symbol black) is reversed into an exaltation of their essential vitality as *les hommes de la danse,* men of life in direct communion with nature.

22   the earth as source of energy and of life. The image recalls the Greek myth of Antaeus who withstood Hercules by touching the earth to regain strength; it derives here from the African belief in the organic bond between man and the earth (tellurism).

Le totem

The totem is the poet's authentic self and most profound being, which he must disavow to be accepted into Western society.

3   *animal gardien:* a reversal of the notion of guardian angel.

4   *le barrage de scandales:* an open avowal of his natural affinities would be a violation of the condition of his acceptance.

Que m'accompagnent kôras et balafong

This poem is an ode (*woi*), a solemn chant celebrating the past and lamenting its passing. It is also a lyrical exploration of the poet's personal situation, an individual reflection of the distress of Africa in contact with Europe. In its double theme, the poem is determined by the conflict between the two worlds of the poet's experience, Africa and Europe, the former seen in terms of its past nobility and present innocence, the latter at a moment of historical tension. Through his consciousness of this conflict the poet expresses his vision of a new world, a perspective of fulfilment for the African.

The opening lines show him in Europe at the outbreak of the Second World War. The first six lines combine the image of an idyllic landscape in Europe with a recollection of his youth, thus identifying the two. The mood established, his meditations turn upon his childhood and his background, and retrace his subsequent spiritual adventure. In stanza II he recalls schooldays in Africa and first contacts with Western civilisation, which shaped his development, and caused progressive alienation from his own culture. Stanza III conveys his sense of division; against the background of the European crisis, he arrives at an awareness of his racial and spiritual affinities, which leads him to affirm his fidelity to his race and to its cause. In stanza IV, he returns momentarily to his immediate situation in Europe; the mood is bitter and ironic; he contrasts Western culture, which is literary, effete and artificial, with the more vital and fully felt traditions of his own African background. He proclaims the authentic nobility of his people and continent.

Stanza V is a transition from personal meditation to the theme of celebration. He evokes his social and historical antecedents before the intrusion of the white man: the stanza gives a pageant of the African past. He returns to the theme of conflict in stanza VI, which re-enacts the conquest; the elegiac element in the poem begins to sound in the second part of this stanza (beginning with l. 84) when he celebrates dead ancestors and past heroes. This celebration modulates into a heroic mode, developed in stanza VII, largely a praise song to Africa, depicted symbolically as a black princess. Stanza VIII is a more personal expression of the sense of his mission to his race, and his vision of a new African destiny. Stanza IX ends the poem on an intensely lyrical note, evoking night in its essential mystery; this defines his feeling for the special beauty of Africa and his imaginative apprehension of the universe.

The poem covers a wide range of mood, and gathers up in a sustained expression Senghor's themes and preoccupations in the volume *Chants d'ombre*. In its references to the Second World War, it anticipates *Hosties Noires*. The style is varied, and takes in all the features of the previous poems in the volume, from the ceremonial grand manner, reminiscent of Claudel, to the more intimate lyricism of the evocations.

Title: kôra: stringed musical instrument akin to the European harp; *balafong:* African type of xylophone.

Dedication: René Maran: French Caribbean novelist, 1887–1960. His novel *Batouala*, published in 1921 won the *le Prix Goncourt*, and contained the first direct attack on French colonial policy in literature. Senghor considered him a precursor of Négritude.

Stanza I

1   *la rivière:* the Mayenne river. The poem was written in Château-Gontier in the Mayenne Department, south-west of Paris.
2   *Un paradis...deux épées:* after the expulsion of Adam angels guarded the gates of Paradise with flaming swords. The spot depicted is a haven of peace, protected by the river and the guardian, who is the poet's lover (as the last line of the poem makes clear), to whom the poet attributes the innocence and sharpness of vision of the child.
5   The Second World War had just broken out.
    dakhâr: tamarind tree.
8   *Fontaine de Kam-Dyamé:* wells in the vicinity of Dyilôr, where the poet spent his childhood.
10 *pâtre:* shepherd, who also plays the flute in European pastoral poetry.
11 *tann:* sandy plain on the Senegalese coast, where social gatherings (e.g. dancing) are held.
12 *théorie:* poetic word for procession.
13 *tirailleurs:* African riflemen from the French colonies, employed in combat on the Allied side in both world wars.
    chéchia: military cap of the *tirailleurs.*
    aphones: medical term for 'voiceless'; here, 'hoarse'.
14 *Téning-Ndyaré et Tyagoum-Ndyaré:* the poet's twin sisters who both died very young.
    cuivre d'outre-mer: the dead in Serer mythology are thought to be light-skinned or 'copper-coloured'; the poet's dead sisters are seen in this aspect.

Stanza II

15   *l'ombre étroite des Muses latines:* the study of Latin literature brings him in contact with the pastoral tradition of Europe with which he is now dissatisfied.
16   *Ngas-o-bil:* village near Joal where Senghor first went to school with Catholic missionaries.
7–18   a reference to his habit of running away from school.
18   *Fontaine des Eléphants:* a pond not far from Ngas-o-bil, a watering place for elephants.

20 *Verdun:* the town north-east of Paris where a bloody battle was fought in 1916 to halt the German advance on the French capital.

21 the loss of the joys of his youth, now a thing of memory.

23 *le Psalmiste:* King David, to whom the Psalms in the Old Testament are ascribed: in his youth a shepherd and harpist.

24 *Ndyagâ-bâss! Ndyaga-rîti:* nonsense words of a children's song.

Stanza III

27 *Toubab:* French-African term for 'white man'; the poet's mother stresses her son's alienation as a depersonalised man.

29–35 the poet torn between the claims of Africa and Europe, represented by the two women; l. 35 is a warm expression of Senghor's theme of unity.

36–40 see Introduction, p. 36.

38 *corps dépouilleé:* the body as expression of the soul; to be his natural self, the poet has to divest himself of the trappings of Western culture (see also l. 111).

41 *la lointaine trompette bouchée:* the muted jazz trumpet of the American Negro (cf *l'angoisse bouchée de tes larmes* in 'A New York', l. 30).

42 *Comme l'appel du Jugement:* the trumpet in the previous line suggests the trumpet waking the dead on the day of Judgement; the gathering war in Europe is thus represented as Ápocalypse (see l. 129 below).

Stanza IV

46 *Mes agneaux:* Senghor was *professeur de lettres* in the *lycée* at Tours; he sees himself as black shepherd of white lambs.

49 A sardonic restatement of the idea in 'Le totem'.

51 an anterior state of grace recalled by this dream of an organic infancy, deriving from the enduring innocence of Africa.

Stanza V

55 *Dyakhâw:* capital of the old Serer kingdom of Sine later absorbed into the administrative region of Sine-Saloum.
superbe vassal: though reduced to the status of a vassal by the French, the Serer king remains unsubdued in spirit. *Superbe* here has its etymological sense of 'proud' (Latin *superbus*).

57 *dyoung-dyoungs:* royal drums, which accompanied epic recitals of traditional history (hence *le bruit de ses aïeux*).

60 *la conque éloquente:* shell used in divination.

61 *Tokor:* literally, 'Uncle'; a term of affection and reverence.
lévriers à grelots d'or: hounds with bells around their necks used to send messages. In the old Sudanic kingdoms, messages were more commonly sent by a messenger with a staff (*récade* see l. 108).

62 *Pacifiques cousins:* relatives who lived in peace.

63 *Bouré, Boundou:* regions in eastern Senegal once famous as sites of rich gold mines.

64 *chevaux du Fleuve:* a special breed of horses, found in the region of the country's principal river, the Senegal (hence the capitalisation).

65 after the past glory, the anguish of the present, like the evening of a brilliant day.
   l'ombre violette: twilight.
   khalam: four-stringed instrument somewhat like a guitar.

Stanza VI

66–7 Senghor uses the belief in the reincarnation of successive generations in the same
   family (see 'Nuit de Sine', l. 15) to express the relationship of his individual poetic
   sensibility to the collective memory of his people. The idea is developed in ll. 78–83.

67 *Gâbou:* a region in Guinea-Bissau from which the Serer are reputed to have migrated
   to their present home.

68 *Droit dressé:* the enjambement and alliteration express the physical aspect described.
   Fouta-Djallong: a region in Guinea, the site of an old Fulani empire which gave its
   name to the range of hills where the Niger has its source.
   Almamy: Fulani religious chieftain.

72 *sève païenne:* as opposed to the Western, Christian doubling of his African essence.

73–8 A reference to the war between the original Malinke inhabitants of the Fouta-
   Djallong and Fulani invaders, which resulted in the defeat of the former and their
   emigration into Senegal where they settled along the Sine and founded the kingdom
   of that name.

73 *tabala:* war drum.

76 *Seize ans le crépuscule:* recalls l. 65; the sixteen years of war which brought about the
   decline of the empire.

77 *marigot:* marshland.

78–83 Senghor suggests a correspondence between his individual cultural plight and that of
   his ancestors, forced to renounce their household gods and their traditional authority by French conquest.

80 *Les captifs colonnes de ma maison:* domestic slaves, usually captives from war; *colonne*
   means 'procession'.

82 *kintar:* Arab equivalent of one hundredweight (112 imperial pounds).

85 *la Chantante:* again, the African essence, which sings in his veins and animates him.

88 *Sîra-Badral:* Queen Mother who led the Malinke emigration and established the
   ruling dynasty of Sine.

89 *Qui sera la sel:* who will be remembered as the 'salt' of the Serers. The line echoes the
   biblical image 'salt of the earth'.

Stanza VII

90 *Elé-yâye:* 'Mother' in the Serer language.

104 The Princess is a total incarnation of her people; like the symbolic woman in
   'Femme noire' she is a mother-figure associated with the continent of Africa (l. 103).

91 *pédants:* Europeans.

94 the princess as source of moral and spiritual sustenance; the metaphor extends to the
   following line to emphasise her quality as the principle of life.

96 *tata:* fort.

100 *au visage d'ombre...:* the contrast between the black face of the Princess and the
   whiteness of her teeth furnishes this brilliant image (see also 'Taga de Mbaye Dyob',
   l. 12).

104–6 For the significance of blood in the symbolism of Senghor, see Introduction, pp. 24–5.

106–7 the Africa of the future seen as the organic unification of all her peoples.

Stanza VIII

108 *récade:* staff of authority, usually made of ivory; the poet hopes to be an emissary of his people, as he calls himself in a poem in *Ethiopiques:* 'Ambassadeur du peuple noir'.

109 *Gongo-Moussa:* an emperor of ancient Mali, who made a memorable pilgrimage to Mecca in the fourteenth century.

110–14 Like Christ who fasted 40 days in the desert before starting his mission, the poet will make an ascetic retreat to prepare for future action.

113 *méhari:* a breed of fast camel.

115 *Mais je vous laisse Pharaon:* although the poet's pilgrimage takes him through Egypt, (l. 114) he does not wish to press his claim on ancient Egyptian civilisation, considered by European historians as white.

mon *arrière-grand-père aux oreilles rouges:* an allusion to a European ancestor. The family name 'Senghor' is derived from the Portuguese *senhor*.

116 *hyperboréens:* Hyperboreans were, in Greek mythology, a race of happy men inhabiting a region of sunshine and splendour somewhere north of Europe.

117–20 *Cette colonne solennelle* echoes l. 80. The new assembly is of free men, Africans reborn to their authentic heritage.

117 *mithkal:* Arab gold weight.

119 *épaules musicales:* graceful, harmonious; see also *visage mélodieux* in l. 147.

126 *amphore:* from the Latin *amphora*, Roman vase with two handles, of elegant design.

Stanza IX

129 an allusion to the war in continental Europe. The Somme, to the north near the Belgian border, the Seine in the Parisian region, and the Rhine, to the east, are rivers in France; *les sauvages fleuves slaves*, probably the Danube and rivers in Eastern Europe.

sous l'épée de l'Archange: recalls l. 2 and l. 42; the war is seen as divine punishment.

132 *Toko'Waly:* see Introduction, p. 2.

137 See 'Lettre à un poète', l. 20.

140 *Taureau, Scorpion*...The signs of the Zodiac, in African terms.

142 *l'intelligence de la déesse Lune:* the moon is the expression of night and symbolises the poetic values of Senghor's Négritude (see also ll. 150–1).

145–8 See 'Femme noire', ll. 2 and 17. There is a total fusion in this evocation of the sculptural image with the idea of landscape; the passage represents an invocation by the poet of the sources of his inspiration, Africa as Muse.

145 Note the progressive build-up of the image with the alliterations in the second part of the line.

150–1 night as the period of the day that accords with his African essence, symbol of the values on which his being is founded.

153 This line connects with l. 2; in his return to his sources, the poet associates his white lover whose company at the beginning of the poem starts him off in his meditations, and whose individual quality renders her apt to accompany him.

A l'appel de la race de Saba

In 1936 Italy, under the Fascist government of Mussolini, invaded Ethiopia (or Abyssinia, as it was then known), and reduced the empire to the status of an Italian colony. This was an important stage in the chain of events that led to the Second World War.

The Italian occupation of Ethiopia had a particular significance for all black intellectuals; it was another flagrant expression of the contempt of Europeans for the coloured races. Ethiopia, the seat of an ancient and prestigious monarchy which traced its origin back to the Queen of Sheba, became a symbol of all Africa, of her historical plight and of her desolation.

Senghor wrote this poem, appropriately styled *woi* (lament), as an immediate reaction to the event. He brings together the elements of his anti-Western feelings as they were developing. Although an expression of a public sentiment, dictated by a political tragedy, Senghor has introduced into it the personal testimony of an individual conflict.

1 *Mère, sois bénie:* an invocation which recurs at the head of each stanza. Primarily to the poet's mother, it applies to the African continent, in her moment of distress. The poem moves between these levels in a continuous shift, expressing the poet's personal involvement.

   This first stanza also contains an evocation of Ethiopia's plight in images of desolation and death.

2 *silence sournois de cette nuit d'Europe:* opposed to *silence rhythmé* of the African night, evoked in 'Nuit de Sine', l. 4.

3 *Prisonnier de mes draps blancs et froids:* a personal note of exile or illness in images associated with Europe, reinforcing those in the preceding line.

4 *Quand fond sur moi:* personal anxiety amplified into a sentiment of dread, combining the threat of the bird of prey (*milan*) and the bleakness and decay of autumn in Europe (*feuilles jaunes*).

5–6 The falling leaves become black soldiers, Ethiopian warriors defending their land against the Italians. Note the strong sonorities (*tonnerre de la tornade des tanks*) to suggest the harshness of the combat and also of the fate of the resisting Africans.

Stanza II

12 *Je me rappelle les jours de mes pères:* a characteristic mental recall of the memories of childhood.
    Dyilôr: A village between Joal on the coast and Kaolack, further inland on the banks of the R. Saloum. Senghor spent the first years of his childhood here.

15 *chaleur nombreuse:* the warmth of the 'extended' family.

18 *Koumba l'Orpheline:* a female character in Serer folktales.

19 *ficus:* a fig tree.

20 *Fimla:* a village not far from Dyilôr.

23 *la rumeur classique de cent troupeaux:* an analogy with the pastoral countryside of classical literature, for example in the *Georgics* of Virgil.

Stanza III

25   *Je ne souffle pas le vent d'Est:* a harmful wind like the Harmattan from the Sahara. The poet wants to keep the memories alive.

26   the mother's lack of familiarity with Western civilisation, her closeness to the simple ways of the village.

27   *pillards du Nord:* the Moors, who raided the various peoples of Senegal up to the beginning of the colonial era.

28   *chambre peuplée de Latins et de Grecs:* his study, filled with the writings of classical authors.

30–1   an emphatic restatement of fidelity to his heritage through the evocation of African ceremonies of sacrifice and libation.

30   *debout près de l'Aîné:* the poet's elder brother.

Stanza IV

33   *les jours proconsulaires:* the colonial days. The territories of the Roman Empire were ruled by proconsuls. Cf l. 8.

34   *et qu'aboient les chiens jeunes aux Esprits:* dogs barking at night are believed in many African societies to see malevolent Spirits.

35   *et moi…je médite je forge…:* a determined dedication to the African cause.

36   *brouillard sans odeur ni couleur:* the fog of Europe as an image of the gloomy character of life in the West.

37   *le dernier forgeron:* the smith, who worked with fire, is considered in traditional society to be endowed with magical powers. (Cf Camara Laye's *L'Enfant Noir*, ch. 2.)

38   *le Maure et le Targui:* Targui, singular form of Tuareg, a people in the north of Senegal. The Moors and the Tuaregs were the traditional enemies of the coastal people of Senegal before the colonial period (cf l. 27). The poet now calls for unity in their struggle.

39   *Ras Desta:* a general in the Ethiopian army who sustained a resistance movement in southern Ethiopia, employing guerilla tactics against the Italians; eventually captured and executed in 1937.

40   *les avions des marchands:* socialist thinking associated war with capitalism, especially munitions manufacturers.

41–2   A reference to Africans under white rule in South Africa; the total frustration of the African continent is given in these lines.

Stanza V

46   *les forts en thème:* those who shone most in Latin exercises; the brilliant students.

48   *Conseils d'administration:* boards of the business companies; a reference to the collusion of capitalism with the colonial system.

49   *coup de pinard:* strong drink before the attack.
     grigris: talismans, amulets.

Stanza VI

54 *Kor–Sanou:* literally 'Champion of Sanou' or 'Protector of Sanou'; Sanou is an elder
sister of Senghor. Cf 'Ndessé', l. 4.

56 *le paean* (or *péan*): a heroic hymn to the gods of Ancient Greece, contrasted with the
war cry of these combatants. This struggle will have none of the refinement of a
literary adventure, but will be brutal and bitter.

57 *la Marseillaise de Valmy:* the French national anthem, *la Marseillaise,* composed in 1792
after the first victory of the French revolutionary army at Valmy, against the forces of
the aristocratic states in Europe. The poet calls for the same revolutionary ardour.

58 This short line establishes the relevance of the ideas of the French Revolution to the
situation of colonial peoples, hence *catholique* i.e. universal.

59 A roll call of the peoples in the former French Empire. *Terre des rizières* refers to the
peoples of the Far East – of Indo-China, present-day Vietnam.

61 *Le Cafre* (or *Kaffir*), South African; *le Kabyle,* a people in the South of Algeria, the
original inhabitants of that country before the advent of the Arabs; *le Fân,* a people
in Gabon, and *le Fôn,* one of the ethnic groups in Southern Dahomey. *Le Bambara,* a
people in present-day Mali; *le Bobo,* those in Upper Volta who inhabit the region of
Bobo Dioullaso; *le Mandiago,* those in the southern region of Senegal beyond the
Gambia (i.e. Casamance).

62 *le prestataire:* in the system of forced labour once employed by the French in their
former colonies, a *prestataire* had to give a certain number of hours of work without
pay.

64 *le mineur des Asturies:* a mining region in north-west Spain.
Dupont, Dupuis: common French names (like Smith and Jones in England), standing
for the ordinary man in the street.
tous les gars: slang expression, rather like 'all the boys'.
Saint-Denis: a working-class suburb of north Paris.

Stanza VII

67 *camarades, combattants:* terms in the vocabulary of Marxist militants. In this line, as in
the whole stanza, the poet expresses the Marxist ideal of the universal struggle
against capitalism, involving the solidarity of the working classes in Europe and the
colonised peoples.

Méditerranée

This poem is addressed to a friend, recalling a journey in 1932 on a boat from
Marseille to Dakar. The poet travelled third class in the holds, with Senegalese
soldiers being repatriated, and so was able to observe the ordinary folk of his country
more intimately. He evokes memories of the journey and associated themes. His
habitual proccupation with Africa is conveyed in a slightly different register. The tone
is less declamatory, even meditative, and the imagery is so integrated into the
movement of the lines as to give it at times an impressionistic character.

1 *Et je redis ton nom: Dyallo:* in many African societies, a man's name indicates not just
his lineage but his spiritual constitution. The meaning attached to a name derives
often from the circumstances of birth, which almost always determine the name, and

from the attributes with which one is considered as a result to have come into the world. The religious significance of names, representing one's total being, explains the importance of the apostrophe in traditional African poetry, on which this poem is partly modelled. (Cf the opening line of 'Taga de Mbaye Diob'.)

2   *la mi-nuit de nos deux langues soeurs:* the two speak different but related languages.

5   *Almeria:* town in Spain bombarded by German warships in 1937. N.B. the contrast between the 'mouths' of the ships' guns and the smiling lips of the sea.

6   Note the run-on from l. 5, the position of *Eclaboussant,* echoing and emphasising *éclataient.*

7   the short line breaks the movement and acts as a pause before the following evocation. The same effect is produced by ll. 10 and 13.

10   See Notes, 'Kôras et balafong', l. 68.

12   *Timbo:* village in the centre of Guinea, in the region of Fouta-Djallong.

15   See Introduction, p. 27.

17–18   the merrymaking of the African soldiers in the lower decks.

19–20   An opposition is suggested between the vigour of the entertainment from the lower decks and the constrained manner of the Europeans in the upper decks. Cf the contrast between *battements de tamtam* in l. 17 and *dernières mesures du tango* in l. 20.

21   transition from evocation to symbolic writing. The young woman leaning over the rail of the ship contemplates the sea whose depth is its mystery, and dreams of new experiences.

22   *Une grosse étoile montait:* the Morning Star.
    éclairant ton front lisse: the illumination is not only physical but suggests Dyallo's communication with the elements.

Luxembourg 1939

The Luxembourg Gardens are in the Latin quarter of Paris, not far from the Sorbonne. In this poem, evoking the desolate atmosphere of the park at the onset of the Second World War, Senghor expresses the dark mood of the time as well as personal grief at the turn of events. The critical attitude of the black poet, judging the result of Western civilisation and alive to its moral imperfections – seen in the ferocity of the war – begins to emerge clearly here.

2   The central section of the park has a fountain surrounded by a shallow pool in which children sail toy boats. The bare and desolate aspect of the park in autumn symbolises the war just begun.

5   *fermé le théâtre d'enfants:* at the west end of the park is a famous theatre for children. The poet dwells upon childhood, associated with flowering and innocence of spirit, and in ll. 6 and 7 with his own youth and fresh hopes, as a contrast to the tragedy of war.

8   *Les voici qui tombent commes des feuilles...:* The first victims of the war are like the leaves falling from the trees in autumn.

11   *la retraite ruminante des Sénateurs:* the deliberations in the chamber of the French Senate, in the Luxembourg Gardens. The old senators are protected by cannon; the young soldiers are exposed to them at the front by the decisions of the elders (see l. 15).

12   *On creuse des tranchées sous le banc:* preparations for war; in normal times lovers would sit on the benches in the park.

Camp 1940

Directly inspired by Senghor's experience in a prisoner of war camp, this is a realistic description of the conditions of the camp, in itself a *critique* of the European war, with his feeling of the necessity of infusing new values into the life of humanity in order to remake the world (cf 'Neige sur Paris').

Dedication: Abdoulaye Ly: an eminent Senegalese economist and political scientist.

1-3 The first three lines, repeated at the end of the poem, form a refrain like a chanted lament, establishing the mood of melancholy. *Jardin de fiançailles* refers to France; *lilas blancs* and *muguets* are flowers traditionally associated with the French; *muguet* is purple in colour and is gathered in May. These references are a poetical rendering of the expression 'the flower of France'; the best of the nation is now being destroyed. *Muguet* esp. in folksong, conveys the bloom of youth; also the idea of love and union (cf *fiançailles*, echoed in *fiançées*, which suggest the idea of birth and life). An extended metaphor for the folk-life, civilisation and humanism of France, as a background to the savage conflict sweeping through Europe.

Isles de brise...: See 'Lettre à un poète', l. 3.

4 *le pays frais des vins et des chansons:* France. After the defeat in 1940, France was occupied by the Germans who divided the country into two halves (hence here: *de part en part*), established an administration in Paris and ruled the northern half, leaving the south to be administered by a government of Frenchmen, under Maréchal Pétain, with its headquarters at Vichy.

5 *du Levant au Ponant:* from East to West (sunrise to sunset).

6-9 The camp is now contrasted with an African village. The sound effects underline the realism. *Deux fosses de pestilence* (open sewers) leads naturally to the verb *fermentent* at the centre of l. 7, to render the feeling of decay and of death (*été mortel*); *l'immobile hargne des barbelés* in l. 8 expresses the aggressive and hateful barbed wire fence preventing escape; *quatre mitrailleuses* refers to the guns in sentry towers at the corners of the camp.

10 *les nobles guerriers:* the French prisoners. Ironic, given the actions which they are seen to perform.

11 *Songe:* obsession with material needs.

12 *Mais seuls Ils ont gardé...:* the central idea of the poem. The black prisoners are able, by their innate qualities (*âme de feu*), to retain their human nature amid the general degradation.

13 See Introduction, p. 29.

14 *les grands enfants roses:* the French prisoners, reduced to an infantile state by the conditions of captivity. Develops the irony of l. 10, and is linked to l. 12: the moral collapse of the white prisoners is due to their previous lack of spiritual sustenance. The Africans, usually considered inferior and often compared to children by Europeans, reveal themselves under stress to be stronger than their white companions, to whom they now give spiritual guidance and support.

15 feverish anxiety and torment.

16 *Les contes des veillées noires:* one of the principal channels of African cultural and spiritual expression.

les voix graves...silence: the inner quality of the African, solemn and mysterious, in communion with the silent forces of the universe.

The division of this line indicates the twofold aspect of Senghor's idea of
Négritude – on the one hand, the social and cultural manifestation of African
civilisation – the objective form of Négritude – and on the other, the imprint of those
factors within the Africans' soul, their inner expression.

18   *Ce sera pour demain....* a dreamlike sequence, a vision of a new life.

19   an evocation of vast horizons, indicating the boundless limits of the poet's vision.

20–4   The prison camp is transformed into an edenic scene where all nature combines to
lend an air of tenderness and of mystery.

22   *leur visage est bleu-noir:* the stars. This colour-notation has in Senghor's poetry a mystic
connotation (see Introduction, p. 27).

24   *les chemins les invitent à la liberté:* recalls *la liberté de leur âme de feu* in l. 12.

25   *leur devoir de joie:* the African's role is to bring a new joyful inspiration to the world;
cf 'Prières aux masques', ll. 17 and 18.

25–6   *les corvées, les travaux de honte:* military 'fatigues', sanitary duties.

27   *gamelles:* tin cans used as drums to make music; even in captivity, Africans retain
their sense of life expressed in rhythm.

28   the essential nobility of the African and the poet's faith in his destiny.

29–31   The refrain returns the poet to the harsh reality.
Stalag: German abbreviation for 'prisoner of war camp'.

Taga de Mbaye Dyôb

A taga is a heroic chant among the Serer, usually sung to outstanding individuals.
Senghor has adapted the oral form into a praise poem in honour of one of his
comrades in captivity. The controlling idea is that of an authentic honour, merited by
the conduct of the individual, rather than his birth or rank. To the declamatory
enumeration of glorious deeds and qualities in the traditional praise poem, Senghor
adds the warmth of his lyricism, particularly in the second part of the poem from
l. 14.

1   The apostrophe is like an opening chord, the line is an opening formula, as in a
conventional praise poem. Throughout the poem, the name is repeated at key
intervals, forming a ground base on which the eulogies are developed.

3   *Dyôbène:* collective name for Dyôb, of the family of Dyôb (also written Diop.)

4   The cold of European winter, against which the red-hot stove is ineffectual, is a
metaphor for the insensibility to which Dyôb's African warm-heartedness, is opposed.

5   In the conventional praise poem, the subject's genealogy and antecedents are enumerated as an indication of his rank. Dyôb's status would not normally entitle him to
this honour, or to having his praises sung to the accompaniment of a *tama* – a small
drum with which the *griots* accompany praise songs.

6–8   The effect is anticlimactic, almost comic, and reinforces the idea of Dyôb's ordinary
rank. Lines 7 and 8 are anti-heroic substitute for the attributes that a praise-singer
would normally recite.

9   *Honneur blanc:* a pun – honour gained in the service of the white man, over and
above Dyôb's genuine merit.

10   *Gandyol:* village on the outskirts of St Louis, north of Dakar. Mbaye Dyôb presumably
came from there.

12   *un collier d'ivoire de leurs bouches:* the virgins smiling at Dyôb with flashing teeth, and
thronged around him in a circle.

13 The elements participate; cf l. 24.

4–22 *Lors elle chanteront...:* a typical song of welcome by a company of village girls (cf introductory note, 'l'Absente').

14 *les tanks et les avions...sortilèges:* allusion to the common practice in African communities of wearing magic charms as a protection against weapons. The poet is emphasising the omnipotence of the white man's tanks and planes.

16 *marche-pied des griots des bouffons:* the *griots* belong to the lowest caste in the traditional social structure of Senegal. The 'Hebrew superlative' emphasises the humiliation to which Dyôb is reduced in captivity.

17 The action which earned Dyôb this praise poem, is indicated. It appears that he chose to remain with his companions in the camp rather than be set free.

20 See Introduction p. oo for the use of alliteration in this line.

21–2 the sense of community negatively illustrated.

23 *Wâlo:* the valley of the Senegal river, in the region of St Louis.
Ngalam (or *Galam*): in the east of Senegal, the site of a gold mine in pre-colonial days. The line suggests the extent to which Dyôb's honour will be broadcast.

24 Cf. Introduction, p. 35.

25 The repetition of the subject's name in this closing line rounds off the praise poem; the poet announces that he has discharged his duty.

Ndessé

Ndessé is a Serer word signifying sadness, melancholy. (Another poem in *Chants d'ombre,* 'Ndessé ou Blues', links with the American Negro lyrical form.) Senghor in his captivity, invokes his mother, symbolising his country, with a note of sadness arising from his present situation, and set against his memory of an earlier state of grace. The whole poem moves through this opposition of two contrasted pictures, with the poet as the central subject of this development.

1 *l'extrême hivernage:* at the height of the rainy season.

2 *la fête gymnique de tes moissons:* the wrestling matches during the harvest season among the Serer. The imagery to l. 6, develops the atmosphere of a festival in which the poet is presented as he should be, the living symbol for his mother (and his country) of the fullness of the harvest of their care.

4 *Katamague:* the coastal region of Senegal south of Dakar.

–11 a custom among the Serer. The old women in times of disaster would dress up like men, would fire guns into the air and shout vulgar words in deformed French, as magical formulae with which to conjure away the disaster.
paragnessés: a deformation of the word *français.*

12 The poet's estrangement illustrated by the fact that he is now unable to speak Serer properly.

15 *marabout:* a teacher in the Koranic school. In Muslim societies the *marabout* has considerable influence and authority in the community. (Cf H. Kane's novel, *L'Aventure ambigüe.*) The line expresses the poet's humiliation by his captivity.

16 *pattes pachydermes:* the tanks are like elephants in their weight and ruthlessness.

22 Cf 'Camp 1940', l. 16.

Lettre à un prisonnier

Senghor was released in 1942 on grounds of ill-health, and spent the remainder of
the war in Paris under surveillance. This poem written after his release is addressed
to his African companions still in captivity, and recounts his reaction to renewal of
contact with 'civilised life'. The bitterness of his disillusionment with life in Europe is
given a new edge by two years absence. Against the lack of warmth and naturalness,
which Senghor sees in the material civilisation of Europe, he opposes again the
directness and freshness as well as the grandeur of life in his Africa.

1   *Ngom:* Koly Ngom, a comrade in the camp. The other names are also fellow
    prisoners.
    Tyâné is a Serer woman's name. Ngom is here given the praise name of a champion
    wrestler in this apostrophe.

3   *salut blanc; cri blanc:* wan, pale; melancholic.

5   *Tamsir Dargui Ndyâye: Tamsir* is a learned man, equivalent to 'doctor', hence *qui se
    nourrit de parchemins,* spiritual nourishment derived from the study of learned
    writings.

7   *voix est couleur de flamme:* has a double meaning. The traditional Senegalese poet was
    also a singer and musician (*Dyali*), and this phrase refers both to Samba Dyouma's
    'golden' voice and to the passionate, ardent content of his lyrics.

11 a switch to the poet's description of his experience in Paris. (The same expression, *Je
    t'écris* is employed in l. 22 to make another transition.) The image is both factual and
    metaphorical; apart from the solitude of his surveillance, the poet feels his apartness
    as a black man.

12–13 imagery from the technical world of Western civilisation to denote the poet's percep-
    tion of its insensitivity and superficiality, contrasted to the fullness of African life.
    Toute graine sur les masques d'ancêtres in l. 13 is linked to the previous line and thrown
    into relief by its position here, and coupled with a moral attribute in the line. The
    natural grain in the wood of the masks gives them natural strength connected with
    their sacred value. This symbolises the spiritual quality of the African, whose intensity
    is diminished by absorption into the material civilisation of Europe. Cf l. 29 of 'A
    l'appel de la race de Saba'.

14 *qui ne nourrissent pas:* which nourish the body but not the soul.

16 Probably a reference to the political situation in France under German occupation,
    where prominent people shifted allegiances between their fidelity to Free France and
    collaboration with the Nazi occupiers.

18 *Et la Science et l'Humanité...:* ironic reference to Western claims to development.
    aux frontierès de la négritude: the word is used simply as a collective word for black
    people the world over.

21 *vide fait autour de ma peau:* a rare report of Senghor's personal experience of
    racial prejudice. He has just returned from fighting for the people discriminating
    against him.

22 Nowhere else in Senghor's poetry is 'white' given so negative a connotation. Note the
    accentuation of feeling in this line, intensified by the progression in the second part.

26 *foin de toute sécheresse parfumée:* 'enough of the superficial elegance of (Western
    culture)'. *Fruits succulents* suggests natural richness; *sécheresse parfumée* suggests an
    artificial state.

27 *énormes comme le nombril de l'Afrique:* like African children with huge navels, the continent is represented in its lack of 'sophistication'. The navel has significance for Senghor as the image of a vital link.

–30 Is this the function the poet would like to assume?

33 *et les doctes en rient:* the wisdom of traditional Africa, naive to the Western mind, opens up a mental and spiritual universe of profound significance. For *surréel*, see Introduction, p. oo.

35 Conquest of dawn over the darkness, which in Europe generates anxiety (*silence sournois de cette nuit d'Europe* as in l. 2 of 'A l'appel de la race de Saba').

36 *la rosée de l'aurore:* Cf Introduction, p. 23.

Chant de printemps

This poem affords a contrast in the brightness of its atmosphere and note of enthusiasm and hope. Spring comes from the south, therefore Africa: the renewal of nature awakes in the poet a new impulse associated with the remembrance of a loved one, to whom the poem is addressed. Though she too stands somewhat as an image of Africa, and spring, the sentiments she arouses are more clearly defined than those associated with the *femme noire* in the poem of that name. This is a love poem built on immediate feelings, eventually given a wider significance. So this poem prefigures the volume *Chants pour Naët* (later renamed *Chants pour Signare*).

The poem is a dialogue. Stanza I is partly introductory; the poet addresses his loved one in Africa from his European exile, and expresses his exaltation and sense of new life with the arrival of spring. Stanza II is the loved one's reply; she recalls the tragedy of war still being played out, and Africa's involvement in it. The war is thus placed at the centre of the poem. The poet responds in stanza III, and restates his new-found hope by calling her attention to the prospect of spiritual rebirth brought by the spring, and which he connects with the vital values derived from Africa.

Dedication: jeune fille noire au talon rose: probably refers to Senghor's first wife, a West Indian.

1 *le ciel primitif:* cleared of the dark low clouds of winter and returned to its pristine freshness. In the pre-Christian era in Europe, springtime was a period of rites commemorating the rebirth of nature (this idea also governs in part l. 39).

3 To the poet, imprisoned in the house by winter, and shut in upon himself (see l. 11, 'Lettre à un prisonnier') the spring brings new hope of relief.
   émouvant: a pun, using both senses of 'moving'.

6 *mon sang:* the poet's life stream – symbolising also his inner essence – responds with a new movement to the spring.

–12 *écoute...:* the exclamation recurs to mark the rhythm, like a pulsation running through the poet's evocations.

8 See Introduction, p. 34.

9 *cigognes:* storks. The birds spread out their wings like full sails and symbolise the vital energy of the natural world. The migrating birds move north in spring, from Africa to Europe.

12 Note the emphasis on *chante* thrown to the end of the line; the sound values suggest the bubbling of sap in vegetation.

Stanza II

15 The landing of Allied troops in the south of France in 1944, moving northward from the Mediterranean like the spring, marked the final phase of the Second World War; many African soldiers were killed.

18 *plus près de nous:* the city of Dakar was under the control of the Vichy government which collaborated with the Germans. It had to be bombed by the Allies at one stage in the war.
    chacals sans lune: jackals at night yelp with raised snouts, as if at the moon; *sans lune* refers to the gloom of the war. The animal sounds characterise the war as the unleashing of savage passions.

19 Cf l. 16 of 'Ndessé'.

20 *cette longue ligne rectiligne...:* the acute sounds suggest the idea of constriction. Straight lines are 'European' and technological.

21 *aigles-forteresses:* war planes, as they might be described in an African language.
    à pleins sabords: from all sides.

25–6 Like the Tower of Babel.

27 Another Scriptural reference, to the massacre of the first born of the Egyptians during the Great Plague.

Stanza III

33–4 *Ecoute le silence:* silence symbolic of contemplation and of the mystic life, the 'true voice' of Africa.

37 See Introduction, p. 30.

39 *sa voix bleue:* of Africa.

40–50 The significance of spring, the theme of the poem, is explicitly stated. From this point, the poem develops into a procession of sensuous images allied to a cosmic vision, in which the passionate love of the poet is extended in meaning to denote the great renewal of the universe. The loved one is associated with the earth itself, into which new life is being infused, the poet and his loved one becoming a microcosm of the couple earth–sun. The promise of rich harvest, suggested in l. 45, is indicated by the fresh buds coming out in the spring, warmed to life by the action of the sun. *Gonfler, s'épanouir* and *germer* have a symbolism of fertility and sexual love.

Prière de paix

The prospect of peace in Europe brightened with the landing of the Allied Forces in France and the repulsion of the Germans on all fronts. 'Prière de paix' concludes *Hosties Noires*; it is a call for reconciliation and harmony, and is one of the few poems by Senghor that is specifically Christian in inspiration and sentiment (cf the organ accompaniment suggested by the poet). The Latin epigram, taken from the Vulgate version of the Lord's prayer ('as we forgive them that trespass against us') sums up the theme. Although a prayer for peace, it develops into a catalogue of grievances, enumerating the exactions and humiliations suffered by black people at the hands of the white races (cf 'Neige sur Paris').

Stanza 1 establishes the mood of bitterness. The poet, as if at the foot of the altar, offers the sufferings of his race as a sacrifice to God and introduces his prayer 'of peace and of pardon'.

In stanza II, the poet recounts the injustices of the Europeans who have belied the teaching of their own religion in their treatment of Africans. This note is developed in stanzas III and IV, where France is singled out, as having denied its own humanistic ideals in its action overseas. The negative catalogue is counter-balanced by the poet's recognition of some of the benefits of French colonisation. Stanza V returns to the theme of the poem, calling for God's blessing on the white races who bear the fresh wounds of war, and for the unity of all races under the wing of God's peace.

The conflict between the poet's feeling of bitterness and his awareness of the need to transcend it gives an inner tension, a dramatic quality. Tragic in tone, the movement of 'Prière de paix', developed through a succession of long, sweeping lines, gives the poem the gravity of a hymn, culminating in its final assertion of faith and hope.

Dedication: Georges Pompidou: Prime Minister of France, 1962–8, and President from 1969 until his death in 1974; a classmate of Senghor's at the *Lycée Louis le Grand* in Paris during the thirties, and a close friend thereafter.

1 *ciboire de souffrances: ciboire* (Lat. *ciborium*) is the special goblet from which the officiating priest drinks the wine during the Catholic mass. As the mass is a commemoration of Christ's last supper, the poet offers the sufferings evoked in this volume to Christ in remembrance of his passion.

3 *l'Orient jaune:* the Far East, where the Japanese were still holding out, and where African soldiers were participating in the war, especially in Indo-China (present-day Burma and Vietnam).

4 *septante:* archaic term for 'seventy'.

5 This line expands upon the idea in l. 1, and recalls l. 15 of 'Neige sur Paris'.

7 *Haïti qui osa proclamer l'Homme...:* an echo of a line from Aimé Césaire's *Cahier d'un retour au pays natal:* 'Haïti où la négritude se mit debout pour la première fois.' The historical reference is to the revolt of the Negro slaves, under the leadership of Toussaint Louverture, against the French colonists in Saint Domingue, which led to the founding of an independent republic, under the name Haiti in 1804.

Stanza II

11 *quatre siècles de lumière:* antiphrasis; an ironic repetition of *quatre cents ans* in l. 8. European 'enlightenment' has not been 'enlightening' in Africa.

13 *talbés:* Arabic, meaning 'pupil', 'disciple'.

15 *de la Corne de l'Occident...l'Horizon Oriental:* from Cape Verde, in Senegal, the westernmost point of Africa, right across to the eastern coast.

17 African religious art has been pillaged, taken back to European museums and made an object of curiosity on middle class Sunday outings.

18 *Askia:* the ruling house of the Songhai Empire from about late fifteenth century to late sixteenth century.

21 *les mains noires...:* the black man made to do the dirty work of the white man; there is irony in this play on *main*. See also 'Neige sur Paris', ll. 14–18.

23–4 an estimate of the toll taken upon the African continent by slavery, often held responsible for the depopulation of the continent.

Stanza III

29 *brigands du Nord:* the Moors.
ses terres à cannes et coton: the sugar and cotton plantations in the West Indies and southern USA worked by African slaves.
34 A neat reference to the German occupation of France against which the French resisted.

Stanza IV

39 Another echo of Césaire's *Cahier:* 'Ne faites point de moi cet homme de haine pour qui je n'ai que haine.'
41 the French revolutions.
43 A deliberate echo of Claudel's *Cinq grandes odes,* to which the Christian sentiment of this poem is associated. The *Magnificat* from this volume contains the invocation:

Soyez béni, mon Dieu, qui m'avez delivré des idoles...

44–5 One rewarding aspect of colonisation was that it brought together different peoples from different horizons. Thus the Arab, the Malagasy and the Vietnamese (for whom the names in l. 45 stand – in that order) came into contact with the African and with each other under French rule. (See also 'A l'appel de la race de Saba', ll. 59–64.)
46 *coeur catholique:* all-embracing – the sense under the religious sense.
47 *images pieuses:* the masks, condemned as pagan and devilish and burnt by the Muslims and by early Christian missionaries, were sacred for the African.
48–9 An allusion to Jacob's dream in the Bible in which he saw a ladder leading up from the Earth to Heaven. The spirituality of the African, expressed by the masks, leads to the same God as that of the Christian.

Stanza V

54–5 describe the aftermath of the war in Europe.
54 *viduité:* emptiness of the fiancée's life after the loss of her betrothed in the war.
56 *boulimique:* of excessive greed.
60 *L'Arc-en-ciel:* God gave the rainbow sign to Adam in Genesis, after the Great Flood which destroyed the Earth, as an assurance of his protection.

Congo

The river is an image of the energy of Africa and a symbol of the flow of life. The poem begins with an invocation to the Congo as source of inspiration, links the idea of the river to the heritage of Africa, then develops into a reflection on the mystery of human existence.

The second stanza weaves images around the idea of the Congo as a woman (cf 'Femme noire'). The third stanza invokes the Congo as river goddess, as agent of creation and principle of universal life. The poet introduces a personal note in references to his situation and Senegalese background; ll. 12–15 express anguish and longing for creative force; ll. 16–24 echo his nostalgia for the atmosphere and mystery of his native land.

The fourth stanza is more confident, even ecstatic. The poet draws strength from his sense of sharing in the force and mystery of the universe; in the two last lines he affirms the theme of the enduring presence of life.

1–2　A single inverted sentence. The poet in an invocation, asks to be enabled adequately to sing of the power of the Congo. This power he identifies with the lyricism of the *kôra* player, representative of the oral tradition.

2　*l'encre du scribe est sans mémoire:* written records are disembodied and so lifeless; the truest art is realised in an immediate, organic way, as in the oral tradition.

3–5　Note the sexual imagery; the Congo is a woman, source of life, and symbol of creation.

6　*toutes choses qui ont narines:* which draw breath, which have life.

7　*Lamantins:* manatees.
nourrice des moisons: overflowing its banks makes cultivation possible; the river is an agent of abundance.

8　*étrave:* stem of a boat or ship.

9　*Saô:* an ethnic group in Chad.

10　*ouzougou:* a kind of hard wood.
diamantine: oil; cf middle stanzas of 'Femme noire'.

11　The outward composure of the river contrasted to the pull of its undercurrents.

12　*l'Impaludée:* the 'feverish' disposition of the continent – its intensity.
surrection: upsurge; an unusual word, derived from Latin.

13　*de la stratégie des fourmis:* governed by *délivre-moi* and attributed to *l'Homme blanc* in l. 15 – the industry of the white man, mindless business.

14　*potopoto:* pidgin French for 'mud', 'muddy, dirty area'.

15　*chants savonneux:* the slippery rhetoric of the coloniser.

17　transition to the poet's longings for a new image of himself.

18　*l'alizé:* west wind. The subject of *sois* is still the *je* of l. 17.
fuite de la pirogue...: the poet's creative force intimately associated with the elements; image used in the last two lines of the poem to bring out its fundamental theme.

19　*Clairières de ton sein:* islets on the Congo seen as parts of the female body.
gongo: a kind of perfume.

20　*Dyilôr:* Senghor returned to Dyilôr during the holidays from the lycée in Dakar (hence *Dyilôr en Septembre*); Senghor's poetic *royaume d'enfance.*

21　*Ermenonville:* a town in the Oise valley where Jean Jacques Rousseau died. Some personal association seems intended.

23　*néoménie:* festival of the new moon.

25　Cf 'Femme noire', l. 12.

26–7　Cf Introduction, p. 26.

9–34　The lines build up a series of images of brilliance and intensity, followed immediately by a drop in the feeling, expressive of the inevitable hold of death (*gouffre*).

30　*Fadyoutt:* small island separated from Joal by an arm of the sea and forming with it an administrative unit, the Commune de Joal–Fadiouth.
choeurs triomphants: singing groups returning in victory from Joal in canoes to their island village after a wrestling contest between the two villages.

33　*crécelles:* rattles attached to dancers' feet.
cauris: cowries.

35–6　Cf the concluding lines of 'Nuit de Sine'; see also 'Elégie des Circoncis', final line.

The canoe reappearing over the waves symbolises the drama of existence and the perpetual surge and movement of life.

Le Kaya-Magan

A monologue, a heroic evocation of a historical figure – the emperor of ancient Ghana. The poet thus elaborates important spiritual values. The poem draws on the theocratic conception of the role of the ruler in traditional societies. At a secondary level, Senghor introduces some personal identification with this conception, through his position as modern political leader maintaining the continuity with the past – also as poet. The person celebrated is thus an epitome of ancient Africa and a symbol of the ideal poet-politician.

Title: Kaya-Magan: first ruler and founder of the ancient empire of Ghana (larger in extent than the modern state of that name).

1 *la personne première:* as ruler who takes precedence over his subjects, also as direct heir of the original founder of the race, and so its present absolute incarnation. The religious importance of the ruler (in addition to temporal power) is based on this fundamental idea.

3 *distants:* the lions are kept at bay by the magical authority of the emperor.

5–7 The traditional ruler presides over the whole of nature in his realm and is the source of all good; See 'Kôras et balafong', stanzas v and viii. He *is* the 'body' of the country, as fount of abundance.

9 *serpent de la mer:* see Introduction, p. 26.

10 *Très pieux...:* the emperor's devotion to his subjects and their dependants has a religious character. *Les faons de mon flanc* recalls the image in l. 3 and presents the emperor as the shepherd of his flock. See also Introduction, p. 29.

Les Guélowars des neuf tatas: guélowar or *guélwar* means warrior, nobleman. The reference is to Kaya-Magan's military commanders at the nine outposts of his empire.

12 *les quatres portes sculptées:* the gates of the capital city open to the four cardinal points, considered in the following lines. (See also 'L'Absente', l. 6.)

13 *sables de l'Histoire:* ancient desert origin of the people of the empire of Ghana.

14 *d'un bleu si doux:* the inhabitants of the south, where the sun stands in the blue at midday; a mystical presentation of the black race. (See 'Camp 1940', l. 22.)

15 *les rouges du Ponant:* The Red Indians of the Western Hemisphere; the poet credits the ancient emperor with a knowledge of this race of people.

les transhumants du Fleuve: possibly the Moors, migrants for centuries across the Senegal.

17 *vous qui déclinez:* the old people, sinking like the sun.

par mes narines: the people draw life from the emperor.

18 the unified consciousness of the poet enables him to resolve in himself the apparent contradictions of experience; the idea is developed further in ll. 22 and 32.

21 *l'Homme rouge-rouge:* dusky men from the north produced by inter-marriage between Sudanese and Berbers of North Africa, and referred to as 'red' in the African languages which have no separate word for 'brown'.

22 restates the unifying role of the emperor and of the poet.

23 *oiseaux de mes cheveux serpents:* in some African masks, the head is represented with

birds pecking the forehead, to signify abundance. The serpents (the knots of the emperor's hair) reinforce his evocation as source of life.

24 *lait bis:* wholesome, healthy; by analogy with *pain bis*, brown bread.

25 *Maître de l'hiéroglyphe:* ancient Egyptian picture-writing (hieroglyphics) had a symbolic character because of its association with secret religious rites – the emperor's insight into the enigmas of life, his intuitive understanding of the world, and the poet's (see also 'Ton nom ne m'est pas inconnu', l. 12).

tour de verre: the poet's isolation – but glass is transparent so he can communicate – variant of the 'ivory tower'.

26 *croissant de lune:* symbol of the emperor's protective rule.

9–34 The last lines identify the poet with the subject of his monologue. The poet is spokesman of the colonised, defender of their spiritual values, and embodiment of their collective mind. He is also mediator between the races, hence his intimate relationship with the white woman. This makes him specially apt to lead his race to a new order harmonising the immediate oppositions in the world.

31 *pomme cannelle:* custard apple.

32 see Introduction, p. 21.

L'absente

In this poem, Senghor lays claim to the special quality and honour of the poetic calling. He develops his idea of the function of the black poet and his social and spiritual significance. This poem is thus closely related to the preceding one. But here he plays down his role as political leader, and gives primacy to his visionary role.

The 'absent one' is the poetic ideal; in the poem, Senghor gives concrete meaning to this abstract idea. So far as it is a vague longing, it represents a loved woman, so the absent one is the Muse. It is also the poet's conception of the spirit of Africa, which awakens the characteristic nostalgia for a passing way of life: also an intense expectation of future achievement of which the poet is harbinger.

The poem develops these associations through concrete evocations. Stanza I presents the poet in the midst of worldly honours which he rejects for the more enduring ones of poetry. This is elaborated in stanza II, on the poet's insight into experience and the essential life of the world. Stanza III expresses his aspiration to the ideal of poetic vocation, symbolised as the legendary Queen of Sheba, and to a mystical union with the spiritual reality she represents.

Stanza IV presents the poet's longing as movement from deprivation to a vision of fulfilment. The images of aridity and barrenness refer to his experience of Western civilisation (l. 31) but refer also to the normal order of nature. In the second part of the stanza, the poet presents in contrast a new season of growth. Stanza V takes up this new theme and associates the images of spring with the symbolic embodiment of Africa as the female figure announcing the new spiritual dispensation. In stanza VI, the poet pays homage to this figure and rededicates himself to his mission as spiritual guide. This leads to the triumphant declaration in stanza VII of the visionary role of the poet who is at the core of human experience and is mediator of the ideal life.

1 *Jeunes filles aux gorges vertes:* the young maidens sing with the joy and fresh vigour of youth.

plus ne chantez: an imperative, and an archaic or formulaic inversion suggesting a traditional kind of address.

l'Elancé: a praise epithet from wrestling, 'the supple one'.

2 *le Lion vert:* Senghor's election symbol in his political campaigns, combining the symbols of his ancestral totem (see 'Prière aux masques', l. 5) and his poetic preoccupation with spiritual growth.

3 *vêt:* from *vêtir*; the poet's head is not covered with gold ornaments, signs of noble standing and worldly ambition.

4 *mes mains si nues:* the poet offers no material benefits.

5–6 *le Fondateur:* is connected to *la ville aux quatre portes* (for which, see Notes, 'Le Kaya-Magan', l. 12).

7 *le Dyâli:* another, more elevated, designation for *griot*, praise-singer, poet.

Stanza II

8 *en allée:* 'who is gone', 'who is away.'

9–11 Note the repetition of *ma gloire*, first as rejection of *worldly* honour, then as statement of the poet's true role; l. 10 is a pure alexandrine, used as a central device in the versification to underline the statement.

9 *stèle:* monument with inscription.

12 *mousse:* moss or fern.

élyme: lemon grass.

13 The progression in the imagery of this line expresses a vision of the universe. *Poussière des vagues*, suggests immense expanses both of desert (suggested by *sables* in the preceding line) and sea. The poet's spirit then rises (the flight of the seagull) towards the illumination of the dominating heights (*la lumière des collines* recalls *du haut d'un haut col calciné* in 'Femme noire'); l. 25 suggests the significance of the hills.

14 *Toutes choses vains sous le van:* all things insubstantial, separated out in a sieve (*van*). Cf St John Perse, in *Exil:*

Toutes choses vaines au van de la mémoire.

Stanza III

17–21 dramatic representation of the poet's anxiety, religious in character, for union with his ideal.

20 *les plaies du crucifié:* of Christ.

21 *et je meurs de ne pas mourir:* direct quotation of the Christian mystic, St Theresa of Avila.

24–5 The return of the Queen of Sheba, symbolising the spiritual essence of Africa, and assimilated to the poet's mystic idea, has the same significance as the Christian gospel (*la Bonne Nouvelle*), and is accompanied by an illumination of spirit.

25 *pistes ferventes:* literally, the burning desert, but with a sense of fervour.

chameliers au long cours: the length of caravan journeys and the endurance of the camel.

Stanza IV

27   *Jeunes filles aux seins debout:* recalls l. 1; association of vitality and renewal with the feminine principle.

29   *trigonocéphale:* poisonous reptile of the scorpion family.

30   *pruine:* fine white dust on fruit.

     élytres: the hard wing-case of an insect, especially the beetle.

31   contrast to the idea in 70–2.

32   *citernes:* wells in the desert.

33   The *rejet* gives emphasis and provides a transition.

36   *mitan:* central point; cf *solstice de Juin* in l. 49; both are variations on *Midi* and *Eté* as used in 'Femme noire', l. 4.

37   *flave:* yellow; from the Latin *flavus*, which gave the regular French word *fauve* (l. 51). *cassia:* calabash plant. *cochlospermums:* a flower which grows in the savannah regions of the Sahel.

Stanza V

41   *Sa venue:* of the Queen of Sheba; cf l. 24. *rougiraient:* the future of indirect speech; the coming is foretold for the time when the fire of village councils (*palabres*) will have lighted up in various sectors of society.

42   *lamarques:* landlords; a word forged by Senghor from the Serer *lam*, 'land', and the Greek *archos*, 'lord', 'proprietor'. *indivis:* judicial term for property jointly owned.

43   *vendus à l'encan:* sold at auction. *pool charbon-acier:* multi-national organisation, typical of Western capitalist society.

49   *Au Solstice de Juin:* at the height of summer.

50   *mirages:* the fugitive character of the poet's vision, which is nonetheless real and substantial (hence *grave des essences*).

51   *fauve:* the bright complexion of the Ethiopian, and the wild majesty of the lion.

53   *pentagramme:* star with five corners, the seal of Solomon, original ancestor of the Ethiopian dynasty, as husband of the Queen of Sheba.

Stanza VI

54   *féal:* fief, subject.

55   *dément de son charme:* ardent admirer; the word *charme* is used here in the strong sense of magical power; the poet's enthusiasm is a kind of madness (the pentagram had magic properties).

57   *horizons de verre:* clear perspective of the poet's visionary future (cf. 'le Kaya-Magan', l. 25).

58   *Mûrisse dans la vôtre:* connect to the subjunctive of the preceding lines; *que ma voix mûrisse dans votre memoire.* *comme la farine futile:* like yeast, apparently insignificant, but giving essential nourishment (cf 'Prière aux masques', l. 16).

59   *Donc je nommerai:* the power of the poetic word to create imaginative realities.

)–3   Note the parallelism of these lines.

62   The enigmatic quality of the poet's ideal. (Cf Notes, 'Le Kaya-Magan', l. 25.)

64   *qui monte à la nuque:* which needs to be grasped by intuition rather than articulated.
65   *le savoir:* the cold knowledge gained from books.
66   *par les mains du kôriste:* creative art as the ideal medium of spiritual life.
69   *colombe-serpent:* plumed serpent, mythical animal combining the attributes of bird and serpent and endowed with special visionary powers. Cf the novel by D. H. Lawrence.

Stanza VII

71   A glorification of the emotional and the intuitive. (See Introduction, pp. 22–5; compare also 'Princesse ton épitre' ll. 37–8.)
74   *qui naît des cendres de la Mort:* a central idea of Senghor; cf 'Elégie des circoncis', final line.
78   *feu sans poussière:* pure flame: the poet's word alone has the enduring quality of essential truths.

A New York

The situation of the black man in America is for Senghor an important part of his conception of Négritude which embraces the black race throughout the world. The historical relationship of black and white is strikingly illustrated by the place of the black man in American history and society. Senghor also sees the black man in America as a living part of the African heritage, sharing an essential African quality.

The city of New York provides an image of the pressures of industrial civilisation with which the black man is confronted in his contact with the white man, yet in which he maintains his identity and brings the promise of a new mode of life. New York is contrasted to the simple natural world of traditional society, with whose values the black man is identified. This contrast is sharply delineated, yet a dominant theme is the necessary reconciliation between the races, and the need for harmony between the two ways of life.

Stanza I is an evocation of the city of Manhattan, presented as a harsh jungle of material living devoid of spiritual comfort. Stanza II shifts the scene to Harlem, the Negro quarter, a centre of exuberant and intense life: what Manhattan lacks, Harlem appears to possess. The final stanza combines the plea for unity with the poet's theme of black renewal.

Stanza I

1   *grandes filles d'or:* prospect of sunlit skyscrapers.
2   *ton sourire de givre:* frost carries the idea of coldness and hardness with the notation of whiteness – the city under the winter snow has a symbolic forbidding quality.
4   *yeux de chouette:* the city dwellers mope in the shade of the skyscrapers (*éclipse du soleil*).
6–7   Manhattan seen as an arid landscape in which steel and stone feature as monsters, hence the animal imagery. The lines that follow develop this idea against an implied contrast of natural life and human grace.
15   *feux follets:* 'will-of-the-wisp' – the play of neon lights.
16   The sanctity of life profaned by contraception which defeats the natural procreative purpose of sexual union.

Stanza II

7–18   Note the prophetic Old Testament terms in which the theme of the black man's role in America is introduced. Line 17 is apocalyptic, while l. 18 carries the idea that the black man is a chosen race which will escape the anger of God.

19   the vitality of Harlem, symbolic of the energy of the black man and the centre of true life in New York (see also l. 32).

    les trombones de Dieu: an allusion to a classic of Afro-American literature, *God's Trombones* by James Weldon Johnson, a book of sermons written in the idiom of black preachers and treating mainly of the Last Judgement.

22   the solemnity of Night in Harlem (set against the trivial agitation of night in down-town New York). See also Introduction, p. 27.

23   *la vie d'avant mémoire:* of primordial time; see also 'Ton visage beauté des temps anciens', l. 2.

24   *Tous les éléments amphibies:* endowed with two lives, with a double nature.

25   *les pieds nus des danseurs:* in direct contact with the earth. See 'Prière aux masques', final lines.

29   In contrast to l. 2, the falling snow is here transfigured into a spiritual image.

30   the Afro-American musical tradition, in particular the instruments of the jazz orchestra; *cuivre* and *hautbois* are the trombone and saxophone; *l'angoisse bouchée* refers to the technique of playing the blues through muted trumpet. The music of the Afro-American symbolises the social condition of the black man in America.

31   *Ecoute au loin:* i.e. in Africa, ultimate source of Afro-American identity.

Stanza III

32–4   the references to blood, e.g. in l. 19, given new significance; the white man is urged to receive into his civilisation the tempering and creative contribution of the black culture.

35   reconciliation based on the fundamental humanity of all the races. *Lion* represents the black man (cf 'Prière aux masques') and *Taureau*, because of its aggressive nature, the white man. *Arbre* is a symbol of suffering deriving from the Christian notion of the Cross.

36   the total unity of life and consciousness. See Introduction, p. 28.

37   In the mythology of Serer, the cayman is held to conserve the secrets of the past, the manatee (*lamantin*) those of the future. The line is prophetic in intention; the poet exhorts the Afro-American to consider his prospects of renewal as a return to his African origins.

Comme rosée du soir

This poem and the next come from the *Epîtres à la Princesse*, love poems addressed to the Frenchwoman who became the poet's second wife; they are dedicated to her grandmother, the Marquise de Betteville. Her aristocratic background is suggested in 'Princesse de Belborg'; her Norman origin makes her an embodiment of the European culture of the north, as opposed to the African Culture of the south represented by the poet.

    The indication for kôra accompaniment shows that this poem is lyrical. The feeling is personal, and bound up with the complex relationship between the black poet and the white woman. The theme is the profound sympathy between the two lovers, despite the difference in their backgrounds.

There are four stanzas with a 'coda'. The first is introductory; the second is in the form of a reply to the woman and touches upon the spiritual basis of their relationship. In the third, the historical conflict between the two races is evoked. The fourth stanza resumes the homage to the loved one.

2   *Tagant:* range of hills in Mauritania.

4   *la bosse du grand mâle:* the hump of the camel, considered a delicacy among the Moors.

7   *Grâces pour ton épître...:* a slight archaism for *merci pour...*

9–10   *la neige:* salutary effect of European winter; the reference to snow is more positive here than in 'Neige sur Paris'.

11   *pays de sel:* Africa, where, for the poet, life reveals its full savour. See 'Kôras et balafong', l. 89.

13   *ta bonté marine:* i.e. deep as, and related to, the sea, on which lies the province of Normandy, the region of France from which the woman comes. The Normans originally came to France from Scandinavia, land of fjords, snow, and fir-trees.
fjord: creeks running inland from the sea in Scandinavian countries.
le sapin qui reste vert: the fir-tree, unlike most trees in Europe, is evergreen and does not shed its leaves in winter; its perpetual freshness is thus an apt image for the enduring beauty and other qualities of the lover.

17–23   See also 'Kôras et balafong', stanza VI.

19   *désarçonnés:* literally, 'thrown off their horses'; metaphorically 'confused', 'dumbfounded'.

20   i.e. the warriors fall in battle with full honour.

21   *cactées:* cactus; *khakham:* thorn tree; both symbolic of the land after conquest.

24–5   the most explicit statement in Senghor's poetry of his spiritual exile, felt as inherent in the political subjugation of Africa.

33–5   Images of the sea, of the north, allusions to her ancestry, beauty and nature.

36   *misaine:* foresail; cf *bonté marine* of l. 13.

41   *Sang de poulain:* denoting physical excitement.

Princesse, ton épitre

The central piece in the *Epîtres à la Princesse*; it illustrates the extension of the love theme into the poet's preoccupation with race. It presents more explicitly than 'Comme rosée du soir' the involvement of the poet's African background, experience and viewpoint with his individual relationship to the foreign woman.

In an introductory passage of seven lines the poet's settled heritage of life and expression are briefly presented, and set against the apocalyptic evocation of Europe's impact on the world. The second part recollects the loved one through whom the poet feels an attachment to Europe in anguish; the poet dwells on pleasant memories of Europe with which she is associated, and invites her to his homeland, pictured in idyllic and elemental terms. Here, Senghor develops fundamental ideas in his conception of Negritude as distinctive way of life; the final lines gather up these ideas and apply them to the poet's feeling for the loved one in elemental imagery.

It is an invitation to share a unique vision of the world.

1   *au coeur des pays hauts:* the Fouta-Djallong region, east of Gambia and on the border of Senegal with Guinea.

2   *les hôtes héréditaires:* these are Fulani (Peuls) to whom Senghor is related on his mother's side (*moitié de mon sang*) and who are generally of fair complexion.

3   *21 rue Poussin:* where the poet often went as a visitor.

4–6 The language described is Peul or Fula, which is spoken principally in the Fouta-Djallong region, and variants of which are spoken across the savannah region of West Africa and into Sokoto State in northern Nigeria. The passage reflects Senghor's feeling for language as poet and as trained grammarian.

5   *sur trois tons:* most African languages are tonal.
    homéotéleutes: technical word in traditional grammar and rhetoric for similar endings of a series of words.
    coups de glottes: glottal stops.

6   *parcimonieuse:* spare, economical. The language reflects the peasant character of the people who speak it.

7   *dévider:* unravel, solve.
    énigmes: riddles, the art of which is widespread in Africa.
    euphuïsme: euphuism, a literary language where terms are expressed in elaborate equivalents. A European term applied to African uses, which suggests that verbal art is both peculiar to peoples and shared by them. The whole letter is written in an elaborate style.

8   *au coeur gauche:* a tautology to emphasise the overwhelming effect of the letter on the poet.

9   *coeur sans parasites:* i.e. free from care, not irritated by (mental) itchings: a euphuism.

10–19 technological civilisation presented as an ominous event presaging spiritual disaster (l. 13). Note the way in which the versification develops into long prose passages.

10–11 aeroplanes defying the laws of nature.

15 This line summarises the devastating effects of the European Age of Discovery upon non-Western peoples, especially Africans.
    une pièce de Guinée: a pun on the English 'guinea' which was a golden coin.

16 *l'an de la Raison:* reason ironically presented as the arch value of Western civilisation, constantly betrayed in action.
    de leurs yeux: an echo of l. 14; refers to the aeroplanes, described in l. 10 as *tigres*.
    ganglions: the constraints of the European intellectual tradition on the free play of the human soul seen as a slave's collar which has grown into the flesh.

17 *on décora...:* the line is ironic; honour is showered upon scientists who design means of mass destruction.
    tuer deux fois l'homme: not only 'more effectively', but also spiritually as well as physically.

20 *Septentrion:* the north, Europe (as opposed to *Midi*, Africa).
    J'ai offert mes yeux: an allusion to the poet's captivity during the Second World War.

21 *rue Gît-le-Coeur:* a street in the Latin quarter of Paris.

23 *Assise:* Assisi, town in Italy, birthplace of St Francis, who founded the Franciscan order of Friars and was reputed to be able to converse with birds and animals.

25 *Montsouris:* park on the outskirts of Paris, opposite the *Cité Universitaire*, the residential campus of Paris University, where Senghor lived for some time as a student.

Tuileries: park by the Seine, the river that runs through Paris. The *Tuileries* adjoins the *Louvre*, the ancient palace of the French kings.

26 *mon obélisque:* the famous monument in the centre of the *Place de la Concorde*, the most important square in Paris. The obelisk was brought from Egypt by Napoleon, and is thus a product of an ancient African civilisation; the poet asserts his direct right to it.

27 The words echo those of Christ asking his disciples to cut all their earthly ties and to follow Him.

31 *la mésopotamie:* i.e. the land of the rivers; reference to Sine–Saloum.

32 *ils ont neuf noms…:* This line recalls ll. 5 and 6; the reference here is to the allusive and symbolic nature of the Serer language.

33 *quadrige:* from Latin *quadriga*, a chariot drawn by four horses in which Roman generals rode in triumph.
   la mitre double: the headwear of the ancient Persians and not of Christian bishops, though with the same idea of consecration.
   ambassadeur de la Nuit et du Lion-levant: combines his association with the black race with his ancestral totem.

37 Lilanga: a Congolese female name.

38–9 Cf Introduction, p. 28.

44 *l'aorte:* aorta, the central artery of the heart, deep into which penetrates the rhythm of the drums.

46–50 In their union, the poet and his love, animated with the pulse of the universe, form part of the cosmic scheme and thus triumph over death.

Je ne sais

This poem and the next are from the section *D'autres chants*. The lyrical quality of the series is illustrated by this one, combining the narration of a personal experience with a song-like approach. The meeting of the poet with a kindred spirit illustrates Senghor's conception of African life as a communion of souls. The meeting epitomises cherished moral and spiritual values.

The poem is like a ballad, with a refrain at the beginning and end (though varied), and the main stanzas forming a narrative with dialogue.

1–2 These lines state the significance of the incident. It retains the enchanted quality of childhood or of existence in Paradise (which are identified, as in l. 3 of 'Kôras et balafong'); so the incident points to continuity of universal life.

3–4 *Fa'oye:* a Serer village not far from Dyillas where the poet's mother was born; *Simal:* a village in the Sine valley; both are locations of shrines. Line 4 echoes the title of the essay 'Comme les lamantins vont boire à la source' appended to *Ethiopiques*.

5–6 In many African societies, malignant spirits are thought to be abroad at midday, when the sun is at its zenith and the heat most intense.

9 *mon poème de paix:* the traditional Wolof salutation, in which the word 'peace' occurs frequently.

17 *sorong:* the Fulani word for the Wolof *kôra*. The clear sharp sound of the instrument is linked to the flashing of the sabre, to give an image of the ideal of honour.

19 *Djenné:* university town and intellectual centre of the ancient Mali empire (hence *vieux parchemin*).

20 The poet's nobility is both of blood and of the spirit.

Laetare Jerusalem

Religious devotion grows out of an individual mood. The poem combines a feeling for nature – evoked at the moment of renewal – with the African sentiment of Senghor. The poem works through contrasts of situation (personal and general) and of references (Christian and pagan) towards the resolution of the final line, which gives an exultant conclusion.

In its self-possession and sumptuous gravity, it offers a contrast to 'Neige sur Paris' another example of Christian expression in Senghor's poetry.

1   *Laetare Jerusalem:* The first words of a passage in the Catholic liturgy for Easter, celebrating the resurrection of Christ. The words mean 'Rejoice, Jerusalem'.

3   *visage d'aurore:* the freshness of springtime at Easter is like the dawn of the year.

4   *l'Eglise au lait doux de coco:* the Christian Church in African terms.

5   *et les femmes de grandes fleurs:* decked out in colourful printed cloth (*pagnes* and *boubous* of l. 6).

7–8 traditional Christian symbols of worship and sacrifice (myrrh and incense) associated with the African.

10   refers to the private agony already hinted at in the opening 2 lines. *Ténèbres* refers also to the 'mourning' services of *Tenebrae* in the days before Easter.

11   *qu'il s'effeuille…:* as the trees which put out new leaves at springtime.

Une main de Lumière

The love-theme is associated with the pastoral tradition (hence the indication for flute accompaniment) and is developed through a series of images whose effect derives from emotional associations, and contrasting and complementary values.

The poem divides into two parts of 5 lines each: the first states the poet's exultant mood as he awakes to the touch of his beloved; the second depicts his devotion to her. The song-like quality resides in the refrain at beginning and end, and in the sound effects.

1   Note the internal rhyme of *lumière* and *paupière* and the contrasting effect of the colour images.

2   *Et ton sourire:* like a dawn. For the significance of *Congo*, see the poem of that name.

5   *fleur de brousse:* i.e. wild, natural.
    l'étoile dans mes cheveux: a poetic notation that complements and reinforces the preceding image of the wild flower.
    pâtre-athlète: the poet.

6   *la flûte:* symbolic of pastoral peace, as in 'Kôras et balafong', l. 10.

7   Note the assonance of *assis* and *cils* (cf *branches* and *bras* in l. 4).
    Fontaine Fimla: a stream in a village near Dyilôr.

8   *mugissements blonds:* synaesthesia; the gentle lowing of the cattle transposed into visual terms.

–10 The variation in the refrain expresses the enduring effect of the loved one on the poet.

Ton visage

The romantic character of the poem derives immediately from the setting: a journey in a canoe along a lagoon under starlight, with the woman chanting heroic praises to the poet. Senghor develops the association (cf 'Femme noire' and 'L'Absente') between the image of woman and artistic expression, and the idea that she is an incarnation of the enduring qualities of the universe.

1–2   Her face suggests an African mask, in its formal beauty and its symbolic association with the timeless values of the race. The identification is made explicit in l. 8, and the symbolic value of this identification in the final line.

3   *Dyônewâr:* a village on one of the islands in the delta of the Saloum river.
bolong: arm of the sea running inland; lagoon.

4   *les ailes des éloges cadencés:* the praise chants rising into the air.

5   *palétuviers:* mangrove trees.

6   the setting is given cosmic resonance, as the heavens and the sea participate.

9   *ndeïsane:* an exclamation of tenderness and admiration.

12   *patine:* patina, the surface quality of a sculpture. Like the mask, the beauty of the woman offers an image of enduring truth.

Ton nom ne m'est pas inconnu

A praise-chant in which the love theme is treated in the heroic mode. The poet insists on the qualities of the loved one which are matched by the power of his art. The expression here is more forceful.

1   *Ton nom:* i.e. the renown of the woman addressed.
Satang and *Sitôr* are the names of her parents.

2   *Pount:* a region of Egypt which produced a rare kind of incense, with opulent associations.

4–10   the strength of character and noble personality of the woman have made her inaccessible to men with resources inferior to those of the poet.

7   *violoneux:* petty musicians.
perles de traite: cheap beads which European traders exchanged for slaves in West Africa.

8   She is as impregnable as a fort.
poussière de sang: the dust stirred by the horses is blood red, and so suggests the ominous portent of the charge.

10   *tout l'art des Peuples-de-la-Mer:* the poet requires exceptional means to win her attention; the line alludes to the art of courtly language as well as the military methods of medieval European civilisation.

11–12   Though she has a secret fascination and mysterious power for other men, the poet's insight enables him to understand her.

12   *hiéroglyphes sur le sable:* i.e. the enigmas of the natural world.

15–16   the eternal significance of woman, a constant element in Senghor's thought.

16   *cailloux, colombes:* the two references, associated by alliteration represent the two poles of Senghor's comprehensive vision of reality (see Notes, 'L'Absente', l. 13)

18   *Dyong:* another name for Joal, derived from the Portuguese personal name *Joâo* (John).

19   *Paroles de poupre:* resplendent, noble language.

Lasse ma tête mienne-ci

The loved one is a source of relief to the poet in his despondency, an idea interwoven with longing for the peace of his native land. The first five lines describe physical weariness and mental depression, the rest show him receiving moral strength from the woman.

1 *ma tête:* the head as the seat of the individual being.
pensées à la chaîne: thoughts like the chains of a prisoner, and in remorseless succession.
2 *taraude:* bore into an object with a screw.
4 *de ma mère lasse:* i.e. weary *for* his mother.
5 *amuissement:* fading away, usually of sound; here, presumably, of the poet's life.
6 The word *sein* is a caesura breaking the line into two even halves; the first evokes the physical contact of the lovers and the second its deeper meaning.
7 *les poissons du rêve:* the sea refers to the depths of the self, and things which rise to the surface of awareness in the dream.
9 *la poupre des vivants:* the couple, ennobled by nature itself, (l. 8) are filled with the fullness and splendour of life.
13 *pommes-canelles:* presumably cinammon.
14 *lait de la lune:* the glow of moonlight, suggestive of the sustaining mystery of night (see 'Elégie des circoncis', l. 1).

Etait-ce une nuit maghrebine?

A meeting between poet and lover, against a background of apprehension. The circumstances of this troubled tryst remain obscure, but much of the poem is given to the description of the interplay between the physical setting and the inner state of the poet. There is no real progression from the dominant mood of anguish to the confident affirmation of the final three lines, but the point of the poem seems to be the supreme value the poet attaches to the woman, who acquires at the end a mythical status.

1 *nuit maghrebine:* i.e. of North Africa (the Maghreb). Mogador is a tourist resort on the Moroccan coast. The poet turns away from artificial pleasures to the memory of his native land (*nuit joalienne*, l. 2).
4 *à l'ombre de notre secret:* the emotion shared by the lovers.
9 *éclairs soudain:* i.e. of the flashing beams from the lighthouse in l. 7.
11 *s'étonnait:* used in the old and stronger meaning of 'being confounded'.
qui n'en pouvait mais: overpowered; *mais* is the archaic form of *plus*.
12 *rafale d'aboiements:* corresponds, in terms of sound, to *éclairs* in l. 9.
13 *mordoré:* light brown.
palpébral: adjective from paupière; the leaves appear to flutter in the wind like eyelids.
14 *dieux géants...:* the guards of the Sultan of Morocco, who were all black. This magnifying of the guards prepares us for the mythical reference of the final line of the poem. Eden here links up with primordial time evoked in l. 3, and also suggests the serenity of the night around, in contrast to the agitation within the poet.
noctuelles: glow worms.
0–1 These lines suggest that the meeting between the two lovers is an illicit one.

22   *Sopé:* term of endearment.
24   *Koumba Tâm:* the Serer goddess of Beauty. The idea in the final two lines is similar to that in the conclusion to 'Ton visage'.

Elégie de minuit

Night usually means peace and repose for Senghor, but the midnight setting in this poem is associated with a mood of dejection and restless solitude. The tone is tragic: a moment of crisis in his life, springing from the discouragement of political responsibilities (as the poem indicates) and his solitary combat against his anguish.

The first stanza suggests the paradox involved in his dissatisfaction with worldly honour and his inability to derive comfort from those values he has cultivated and celebrated as a poet. The second stanza is a dramatic presentation of the poet's distress, countered by his conviction of his inner resources. The third develops this last feeling in strongly sensuous terms, explicitly linked to the poet's habitual eroticism, as well as to its deeper meaning; there is a lapse into the dejection of the beginning, and into a deeper despair. In the fourth stanza, the tone is calmer, the poet prays for the strength of his ancestral values and accepts the coming of the dawn as a sign of new life and peace.

Overt self-dramatisation and the somewhat sentimental conclusion reduce the force of this poem, but it is a notable example of the greater preoccupation with personal themes in Senghor's later work.

 1   *Eté, splendide Eté...:* this invocation stresses the paradox of the poet's situation at the outset, and his strongest aspiration.
 4   *la lumière de minuit:* the spiritual illumination of night, as in 'Nuit de Sine'.
 5   *erg, hamada:* Arabic words for sand hills and rocky hills respectively; the line stresses the flat monotony of the poet's desolation.
 6   *le Père Cloarec:* a Catholic missionary priest tied to a stake and left in the sun for a whole day by the Serer in the early days of evangelisation.
8–9 perhaps his untiring devotion to public duty, which becomes as mechanical as the working of the lighthouse.
10   like a leopard.
     sur le garrot: on the leash.
     Simoun: a hot and violent wind from the desert.
13   *Six mille lampes:* i.e. the poet's books.
20–2 physical experience as the basis for spiritual illumination.
25   The poet in his despair contemplates suicide; the line reinforces his previous wish for annihilation in l. 11.
27–8 These lines give a specifically Christian turn to the poet's agitation; cf 'L'Absente', l. 21.
29   *cette passion de mort et de lumière:* developed in the fourth stanza of the poem.
30   *phalènes:* moths.
31–7 the aspiration in the opening invocation of the poem more fully spelt out.
41   *maladie du sommeil:* the continuous sleeping of the new born babe is a positive sign of its health.
     Marône, Kotye-Barma: two famous traditional artists in Senegal during Senghor's childhood. For the influence of the former, see Introduction, p. 2.
42   *ma poupée rose:* see Notes, 'Neige sur Paris', l. 27.

Elégie des circoncis

The circumcision rite is the essential element in the initiation ceremony which marks the formal passage of the adolescent from immaturity to adulthood. The ceremony involves the confinement of candidates for a time during which they undergo a series of trials and receive instruction in the history and customs of the community and training in the details and values of manhood.

Senghor identifies his progress through life with this custom of traditional societies, and applies its symbolic value to his preoccupation with his poetic vocation. The first two stanzas of the poem evoke the ceremony and its significance; the ordeals of the candidate (involving physical pain and mental stress before his admission to the community of men) represent a transformation of the individual, leading to a more intense life, a ritual death from which he rises fortified. The last two stanzas establish the parallel between this ritual and the poet's experience, and his function as agent of higher reality: the poet's rediscovery of ancestral values brings him a new illumination of the spirit which raises him above the trials of ordinary living and gives him new insight into the essential life of the world.

The fundamental theme is the inner renewal of man; the realisation within experience, individual and collective, of a fuller life in harmony with the forces of the universe. The poet places the source of this renewal in a return to the primary experience of childhood, from which the adult is removed. Poetry restores to life, made drab by everyday preoccupation, that spiritual dimension which gives it value. Imaginative experience purifies the vision and transforms existence, and represents an initiation into a higher order of reality.

1–3   There are three progressive levels of significance in this invocation to night: as scene-setting for the evocation of the initiation ceremony; as nostalgic recall of the poet's early life and antecedents; as symbol of those values that constitute his poetic universe.

4   *enfance extrême:* final stage of childhood; the construction is Latin; cf *l'extrême hivernage* of 'Ndesse', l. 1.
    les rugissements des lions: the simulation of the roaring of lions, part of the initiation ceremony and meant to develop courage in the candidates. Cf Camara Laye's *L'enfant noir*, chs. 7 and 8.

5   *silence sournois:* charged with fear, in this particular context; the usual positive symbolic connotation of silence reappears in ll. 13 and 28.

8   the symbolic death of the life of childhood.

9–10   the representation in nature of the symbolic significance of the initiation, which implies the destruction in the adolescent of all that is immature.

12   *la robe:* the long loose garment open at the sides, worn by the initiates.

13   the ceremonial dance of the initiates after the ceremony to mark their gaining of a new life.

14   note the capitalisation of *Vie* reversing the device applied earlier to *mort* in ll. 7 and 8.

15   *que se lève la nuit du sexe:* initiation also purifies the adolescent in preparation for sexuality, in its creative function.

16–17   the poem as exemplar of the imaginative feeling for the world, which is concerned with essential life. The poet insists on the cumulative symbolic power of the imagination, to which the artifice of its expression is auxiliary.

18–19 See Introduction, p. 25
   21 *Midi-le-Mâle est l'heure des Esprits:* see Notes, 'Je ne sais', ll. 5–6.
23–5 In contrast to the fresh and free spontaneity of childhood experience, adult life is joyless, bare and superficial.
   23 *la règle du compas du sextant:* the limitations of practical living.
   25 *le serpent:* symbol of wisdom, contrasted to *les roseaux*, signifying human beings in their transient, superficial quality.
   30 the ebb and flow of life reflected in imaginative experience; the idea is restated more forcefully in the final line of the poem.
   31 *Maître des Initiés:* who conducts the ceremony and gives instruction in the practical and spiritual aspects of life to the candidates.
le chiffre des choses: the mysteries of the universe.
   32 the civic and moral obligations taught to the initiates.
   34 *Le chant n'est pas que charme:* i.e. the function of imaginative expression goes beyond giving delight and has a visionary significance.
   35 *oiseaux-serpent:* symbolising total knowledge (see Notes, 'L'absente', l. 69). The whole line expresses the idea of imaginative experience as a celebration of life in all its range and fullness.
   36 *Phénix:* mythical bird supposed to rise from its own ashes and thus a symbol of regeneration. The thought and imagery of the whole poem culminate in this line. The poet identifies the essence of imaginative life with the force of renewal in nature. The stripping away of inessentials to give greater force to experience, which the poet prescribes in ll. 16 and 17 is assimilated, in the phrase *le carnage des paroles* to the purifying and strengthening value of the ordeal of circumcision. This is an image of the emergence of a new and stronger life, denoted by *les ailes déployées* (cf l. 9 of 'Chant de printemps'), out of the apparent destruction of the natural world and its renewal, which make the rhythm of the seasons and the cycle of the universal order – in short, the triumph of life over death.

INDEX OF FIRST LINES